D1592098

The Ultimate Daycare Starter Workbook

How to Start a Daycare and Run it Successfully

Written By: Kris Murray

5th Edition

www.DaycareHotline.com

Copyright 2008-2013 Daycare Systems LLC

The content of this publication provides the author/publishers opinion in regards to the subject matter provided herein.

The information in this book, is neither a substitute for any type of professional advice, nor is it an interpretation of laws, rules or regulations concerning the subject matter.

It is strongly suggested by the author/publisher, concerning licensing, registering or certifying a business, that the reader seek the services of the appropriate licensed professional or agencies when necessary.

It is further suggested that the reader comply with all licensing requirements of the community and state in which the business is to be located.

The author/publisher is not responsible for any personal liability, loss or risk incurred as a consequence of the application and/or use, either directly or indirectly, of any suggestions, advice, information or methods presented in this publication.

COPYRIGHT ©2013 Kris K. Murray
Published by: Daycare Systems LLC

ALL RIGHTS RESERVED, UNLESS OTHERWISE INDICATED.
NO PART OF THIS PUBLICATION MAY BE REPRINTED OR REPRODUCED
WITHOUT THE WRITTEN PERMISSION OF DAYCARE SYSTEMS LLC.

The Ultimate Daycare Starter Workbook is dedicated to all the women and men who strive to provide quality childcare in order to make a positive and unique difference in the lives of little ones.

As a mom who has worked part-time since my kids were born, I owe a debt of gratitude to the caregivers of my two children, Owen and Maeve.

Special thanks to my husband Devin for his loving support and advice, and for always being there for me.

Copyright 2008-2013 Daycare Systems LLC

About the Author

Kris Murray has over 20 years of experience in marketing and business coaching, in many different industries. Her mission as the Daycare Success Coach is to help people start and run a successful daycare business, either in a home or a center.

By focusing on specific success strategies that will provide more income & profits, daycare owners can fulfill their dreams of owning their own business while spending the day with children.

Kris is the creator of The Daycare Success System, as well as the owner and president of Daycare Systems LLC. She lives in the mountains of Colorado with her husband and two children.

For more information on the Daycare Success Coach products and services, please visit Kris at www.DaycareHotline.com.

If you want help growing your enrollment and taking your daycare business to the next level, please visit Kris at www.Childcare-Marketing.com.

Copyright 2008-2013 Daycare Systems LLC

TABLE OF CONTENTS

Before You Get Started

This book has been written in easy to use format and is designed for use along with your state's licensing requirements.

Start with the first section, and complete the workbook, as you read, research and make the appropriate decisions, for your daycare.

Complete the sections in pencil, in case you need to make corrections or additions at a later date.

Take notes, and refer to them as needed.

Make copies of all the forms, prior to editing and confirm that all forms contain the information necessary for your state licensing agency.

Contact all the professionals you deem necessary or required by your licensing agency to obtain registration.

Setting up and operating a successful daycare will take preparation.

Not only will you need to prepare your home (or center), you will also need to establish, a daily routine and stay organized.

How you present yourself and how you operate your business, will be reflective of the success you experience.

Once you have finished reading the book, completed the workbook pages and reviewed your State Licensing Agencies requirements, use the Checklist on **page 8** as a guide to ensure you have completed all the steps necessary to open your daycare.

Keep this book where it can be easily accessed for future reference.

How To Get Started

Set Up Checklist

- ☐ **Contact Licensing Agency**
- ☐ **Meet licensing requirements**
- ☐ **Contact Food Program Sponsor**
- ☐ **Complete participation requirements**
- ☐ **Contact Resource and Referral Agency**
- ☐ **Meet requirements**
- ☐ **Contact Bookkeeper**
- ☐ **Complete Business Plan:**
  - **Determine hours of operation**
  - **Determine fees and charges**
  - **Decide what services to provide**
  - **Determine your unique market niche**
- ☐ **Write contract & policy handbook**
- ☐ **Prepare interior of home or center**
- ☐ **Prepare exterior of home or center**
- ☐ **Purchase liability insurance**
- ☐ **Purchase supplies**
  - **Bedding**
  - **Toys**
  - **Arts and Crafts**
- ☐ **Prepare daily schedule**
- ☐ **Prepare evacuation plans**
- ☐ **Copy all forms**
- ☐ **Start marketing & advertising**
- ☐ **Prepare enrollment packets**
- ☐ **Open for business**

Copyright 2008-2013 Daycare Systems LLC

Contact Worksheet

Contact the professionals on the following pages in regards to setting up your daycare. Ask the questions shown and any others you may have.

_____ State Licensing Agency

Each state is governed by it's own Childcare Licensing agency. The phone numbers and addresses for all Licensing Agencies are located in alphabetical order by state, in **Appendix A.**

1) What steps do I need to take to become registered or certified as a Daycare Provider? _____

_____

_____

2) What fees are involved? _____

3) How long is the registration process? _____

4) Where can I obtain a list of rules and regulations regarding setting up and running my home daycare? _____

5) What Food Programs are available in my area?

_____

_____

6) What classes, training or certifications do I need to attend? Are any of these available via the Internet?

_____

_____

_____

7) What Resource and Referral Agencies are in my area?

_____

_____

8) Will there be a home inspection? _____

_____ Food Program Sponsor

Participation in the Food Program, will allow reimbursements for some of the costs involved in serving nutritious meals.

1) What do I need to do to participate in the Program?
_____

2) Do I need to keep my daycare food separate from my family's food?
_____

3) For each meal and snack provided, how much per child, will I be reimbursed? _____

4) Do my own children qualify for reimbursement? _____

5) What paperwork is required? _____

6) Will a representative visit my home? _____

7) Where will classes be held? _____

_____ Child Care Resource & Referral (CCR&R)

Participating in a resource and referral program can offer you referrals from parents seeking childcare as well as the following information:
- Assistance with individual childcare concerns
- Workshops and Training available for providers
- Scholarship information to assist providers in paying for training and accreditation
- Sources for videos, books, toys and equipment, which may be borrowed from the Agency
- Resources regarding health, safety, child development, activities, business development, taxes and zoning.

TIP: The website is located at: http://www.childcareaware.org/en/. Then enter your ZIP Code in the search field and you will receive the contact information for your nearest CCR&R. You can also call them toll-free at (800) 424-2246.

1) What steps do I need to take to participate in your Program?

_____

_____

_____ Hospital, Red Cross, or CPR Training companies for Infant/Child CPR First Aid

Training and Certification may be a state requirement. If not, consider becoming certified for the protection of your own children as well as the children you enroll in your daycare.

1) When and where are the classes held?

_____

_____

2) What is the cost of certification?

_____

3) How often do I need to renew my certification?

_____

_____ Local Health Department

A Food Handler's card may be a state requirement. If not, consider obtaining one for your own knowledge on preparing safe meals.

1) How can I obtain a Food Handlers card? _____

2) What are the costs involved? _____

_____ Local City or County Planning and Zoning Department

1) Are there any zoning regulations which would prevent operating a Daycare out of my home? _____

_____ Renters

Review rental agreement or lease for rules restricting operation of a home daycare. If necessary, contact your landlord for more information and insurance requirements, if any.

_____ Auto/Homeowners Insurance Agent

Your existing home owners and auto insurance will not be sufficient coverage for your daycare business. You can either purchase a separate policy or an endorsement/rider to your existing policy.

1) What type of coverage on my home and auto do I need to provide daycare in my home? _____

2) How much will this extra coverage cost? _____

3) Is it payable monthly, quarterly or annually? _____

4) Will this be a rider to my existing policies or will I need a separate Liability Insurance Policy? _____
How much will a separate policy cost? _____

SUCCESS TIP: We strongly encourage you to purchase a separate Liability Policy. See page 40 for more detailed information.

5) Is there a limit to the number of children that I can provide care for? _____

6) Will I be able to allow water related activities? _____

7) Will my coverage provide:
Defense cost protection form lawsuits? _____
Accidental Injury Medical Payments? _____
Business Income Interruption? _____
Property Coverage? _____
Protection for injuries sustained while off my daycare premises, such as field trips? _____

8) I own a dog, do I need to keep it separated from the children during my hours of operation? _____

9) Will I need additional auto insurance if I transport children? _____

If your agent does not provide the coverage you are seeking:
10) Can you refer me to an agent that offers the type of coverage I am seeking? _____

_____ Bookkeeper or Tax Consultant

1) How much do you charge for Consultations and/or Tax Preparation?

_____

_____

2) What items can I deduct as Daycare expenses?
Make copies of the preprinted Ledgers in the **Bookkeeping Section** to use as a guide when speaking to these licensed professionals. Confirm if all of these expenses are allowed and if they apply to your situation.

_____

_____

3) Can you provide estimated tax payment figures and coupons?

_____

4) How much can I contribute to a retirement account? _____

_____ Poison Control Center

Phone numbers for poison control centers are listed in alphabetical order by state, in **Appendix B.**
1) I'm opening up a home daycare, can you send me an information packet and warning labels? _____
If not, where can I obtain more information?

_____

_____ Attorney

For legal advice regarding the content of your contract and other necessary documentation.

_____ State Police

As a courtesy to parents, as well as your own safety, consider requesting a list of registered Child Sex Offenders in your area. Supply a copy of this list to parents upon request.

Copyright 2008-2013 Daycare Systems LLC

Contact any other professionals that you deem necessary or your state licensing agency requires, to set up and run your daycare from your home.

After reading the licensing requirement from your state, make a list of other agencies or requirements needed to set up and run your home daycare.

Additional Contacts as Required by State:

Name: _____

Number: _____

Address: _____

Reason for Call: _____

Notes: _____

_____

Name: _____

Number: _____

Address: _____

Reason for Call: _____

Notes: _____

_____

Name: _____

Number: _____

Address: _____

Reason for Call: _____

Notes: _____

_____

Name: _____

Number: _____

Address: _____

Reason for Call: _____

Notes: _____

_____

Copyright 2008-2013 Daycare Systems LLC

Licensing Regulations

Each state licensing agency creates and maintains it's own list of rules and regulations. Due to the variance from state to state, this book does not contain the regulations for each state. Use this book as a guide in addition to the guidelines provided by your state.

A copy of the rules and regulations for each state can be obtained by contacting the appropriate Licensing Agency. The numbers for each state are located in **Appendix A.**

If a checklist for completing requirements does not accompany your states, rules and regulations, create one using the form on the following page.

This will allow you to complete each requirement, step by step. As each requirement is met, take notes and keep copies of any certifications received, courses completed, inspections, etc. This will assist you in completing the registration process quickly and efficiently.

Create a file to maintain certificates and other state requirements, so they can be submitted to the licensing agency for your state and you can refer to them as needed. When speaking to your licensing agency always take note of the date, the person's name and what was discussed.

During the course of operating your business, you will need to follow the rules of your state licensing agency, if these rules are not followed, you may be fined or lose your daycare registration.

State Licensing Requirements Checklist

- [ ] _____
- [ ] _____
- [ ] _____
- [ ] _____
- [ ] _____
- [ ] _____
- [ ] _____
- [ ] _____
- [ ] _____
- [ ] _____
- [ ] _____
- [ ] _____
- [ ] _____
- [ ] _____
- [ ] _____
- [ ] _____
- [ ] _____
- [ ] _____
- [ ] _____
- [ ] _____
- [ ] _____
- [ ] _____
- [ ] _____
- [ ] _____

Copyright 2008-2013 Daycare Systems LLC

Creating a Business Plan

Start-Up Costs

As with any business start up, costs will be involved. The following example, should give you an idea of what fees you will have to pay and the items you may need to purchase to open your home daycare.

Licensing Fees	$0-$50 (varies state to state)
First Aid/CPR Certification	$30-$50
Liability Insurance	$350-$700 per year (varies)
High Chairs	varies if buying new or used
Booster Seats	varies if buying new or used
Playpens or Portable Cribs	varies if buying new or used
Nap Mats	$7-$15
Bedding	varies if buying new or used
Safety Gates	$20-$40/each
Safety Devices	$10
Computer	$600+
Computer Programs	$10+
Books	$20+
Toys	$100+
Educational Materials	$25+ (monthly if purchasing curriculum)
Arts and Crafts Supplies	$20+
Disposable gloves	$5+
Disposable changing pads	$5+
Antibacterial Cleaners	$5+

Purchase only those items you absolutely need to set up your daycare, buy additional equipment and supplies as needed.

Shopping at resale shops, garage sales or classified ads for toys, and equipment, can help reduce costs.

SUCCESS TIP: BE SURE to KEEP your receipts! Most, if not all, purchases are tax-deductible.

Use the form on the following page when shopping for supplies.

If you have children, you may already own some of these items.

Copyright 2008-2013 Daycare Systems LLC

Daycare Shopping List

Safety Devices

- ☐ Electrical Outlet Covers
- ☐ Safety gates
- ☐ Other _____
- ☐ _____

- ☐ First Aid Kit
- ☐ Disposable Gloves
- ☐ Disposable changing pads
- ☐ Antibacterial cleaner

Equipment

- ☐ Nap Mats _____
- ☐ Crib _____
- ☐ Playpen _____
- ☐ High chair _____
- ☐ Booster Seat _____
- ☐ _____
- ☐ _____

Bedding

- ☐ Blankets
- ☐ Sheets
- ☐ Pillows

Other

- ☐ _____
- ☐ _____

Art/Craft Supplies

- ☐ Crayons
- ☐ Markers
- ☐ Pencils
- ☐ Paper
- ☐ Glue
- ☐ Play dough
- ☐ Finger Paints
- ☐ Paint Sponges
- ☐ Poster Board
- ☐ Water colors
- ☐ _____
- ☐ _____
- ☐ _____

Toys

- ☐ _____
- ☐ _____
- ☐ _____
- ☐ _____
- ☐ _____
- ☐ _____

Other

- ☐ _____
- ☐ _____
- ☐ _____

www.DaycareHotline.com   Copyright 2008-2013 Daycare Systems LLC

Deciding How Much to Charge For Your Services

Contact Providers in your area and ask the following:

1) How much do you charge? _____

   Do you charge different rates for different ages? _____

   _____

   Do you charge when children are absent? _____

2) What type of services do you offer? _____

   Transportation? _____

   Arts and Crafts? _____

   Educational Program? _____

   After Hours Care? _____

   Field Trips? _____

   Do you charge extra for these services? _____

3) Do you offer full and part time care? _____

4) How many children do you care for? _____

Contact Childcare Centers in your area and ask them the following questions:

1) How much do you charge? _____

Age	Part time	Full Time
Infants	_____	_____
Toddlers	_____	_____
Preschool	_____	_____
Before and After school care	_____	_____

2) What days per year are you closed? _____

_____

3) How many children are assigned to each teacher? _____

_____

Copyright 2008-2013 Daycare Systems LLC

Before determining your rates, compare your program, services and hours of operation to those providers and centers you contacted.

The monthly income you generate can vary depending on the number of children in your care and how much you charge for your services.

Determine your rates based on an average of the figures you obtained and the services you choose to provide. Also take into consideration the financial needs of your family, when determining whether to charge by the week, day or hour.

Parents may be willing to pay more to providers caring for smaller groups of children and for extra services, such as transportation, part-time care and preschool and/or learning programs.

A few options to consider in keeping your income steady:

SICK DAYS
Rule of Thumb: Allow a certain number of sick days per year, without charge. Charge 50% of your daily rate, for additional sick days.

VACATIONS
Rule of Thumb: Allow 2 weeks vacation for yourself, without charge, and charge 50% of your weekly rate for each additional week missed.

PAID HOLIDAYS
Rule of Thumb: Charge for certain Holidays per year, even though your daycare is closed. For example: New Years Day, Christmas Day, Thanksgiving Day, Memorial Day and Labor Day.

Whether you charge by the hour, day or the week, get paid at regular intervals, with no exceptions.

Copyright 2008-2013 Daycare Systems LLC

Determining Hours and Days of Operation for Your Daycare.

What schedule will work best for you and your family?
Full time? _____ Part time? _____
Before/After and No School day care? _____
Educational Program? _____
What time do you wish to open and close your daycare each day?
_____

Sit down with your family and discuss this thoroughly before making that decision. Use the form on **page 26** to complete your family's daily schedule. Choose a compatible schedule for your daycare.

Although the majority of parents will be seeking full time care, you may find that a regular schedule of 7:00 am to 6:00 p.m. is not appropriate for your family. You may prefer to provide "specialized care", with limited hours.

There are families seeking this type of care who are willing to pay more for your services, if you can accommodate their schedules.

Examples of "specialized care" are as follows:
- Part-time Care
- Before/After School and No School Day Care
- Educational or Learning Program
- Drop-in Care
- 24 hour Care
- Evening and Weekend Care

When offering "specialized care", consider charging by the hour, at a higher rate.

If you're not sure what hours and days of the week will work best for your family, then try on a temporary basis being open for certain days and hours. If it doesn't work out, then try another.

Keep in mind, if you are experimenting that parents are counting on you and they should be informed up front that you are providing care on a trial basis.

Copyright 2008-2013 Daycare Systems LLC

What Extra Services, If Any, Do You Want to Provide?

TRANSPORTATION

Are you willing to provide transportation to and from school? _____

Do you have adequate seating in your vehicle, for all the children to be buckled in safely (including car seats) ?_____

Does your auto insurance protect you in the event of an accident?
_____

Will you charge extra to cover the costs for gas and insurance? _____

Will transporting disrupt naps, meals, bus schedules? _____

Are the parents willing to pay extra for this service? _____

FIELD TRIPS

Will you be taking the children on field trips? _____

Who will pay the costs of the field trips? _____

Do you have a consent form for the parents to sign? _____

Where will you take the children? _____

Are the field trips age appropriate? _____

Will you have parent assistance at the field trips? _____ If so, what is that parents liability, in the event of an accident? _____

Does your state have any regulations restricting parent assistance on field trips? _____

Does your liability insurance protect you while on field trips? _____

Tip: Create a file to keep in your car, which list each child's name, allergies, and emergency phone numbers, in the event there is an accident.

AFTER HOURS CARE

Will you ever be willing to provide additional care for daycare children Occasionally? Never? Primarily? _____

Do you want to offer Parent's Night Out once a month or occasional overnight care? _____

How much extra will you charge for this specialized care? _____

Will having daycare children in your home after hours affect your family's needs or schedule? _____

What additional state guidelines will you need to follow in order to provide this care? _____

Before offering this service, check with your Liability Insurance Agent and State Licensing Agency, as some restrictions may apply.

LEARNING ENVIRONMENT

What age group do you want to offer this program to? _____

How much will a purchased curriculum cost? _____
  (Note: To check out an example of a top-rated preschool curriculum program, see the Itty Bitty Bookworm at http://www.ittybittybookworm.com)

How much will you charge for this program? _____

If you create your own curriculum, how much time will be involved for planning, preparing and purchasing materials for each activity?

_____

If you are working with a mixed age group, how will you incorporate this program, with the rest of the day's activities? _____

What classes, if any, will you need to take, in order to provide this program? _____

What are your states requirements in regards to offering this type of program? _____

Copyright 2008-2013 Daycare Systems LLC

OTHER PROGRAMS

Do you have special talents you can incorporate into your daily schedule such as musical instruments, singing, dance, art, foreign or sign language or gymnastics? _____

Do you have hobbies and/or interests, such as arts and crafts and/or cooking? _____

Why not use those talents and hobbies to enhance your program?

This will not only provide variety for the children, but will allow you to pursue your own interests.

If you do not want to share your talents or hobbies, why not, bring in a Music Teacher, Gymnastics Coach, etc., so you can include these subjects in your program?

Depending on what type of program you are offering and the area that you live in, you may be able to charge extra for the services discussed in this chapter.

A word of warning, before allowing anyone into your daycare setting to work with the children, be sure to have the parent's consent in writing and proof that those people, have had background checks done. You may also want to collect fees for these activities, up front.

Your state licensing agency may have other rules and regulations with regard to allowing other adults into your daycare home, make sure you are in compliance before offering this program to your daycare families.

Family Schedule

6:00	
7:00	
8:00	
9:00	
10:00	
11:00	
12:00	
1:00	
2:00	
3:00	
4:00	
5:00	
6:00	
7:00	
8:00	

Copyright 2008-2013 Daycare Systems LLC

FIELD TRIP PERMISSION SLIP

_____ (child) has permission to attend the field trip to _____ (place) on _____ (date), with _____ (provider) and any volunteer parents.

Check one:

_____ My child has permission to ride in a volunteer parent's vehicle
_____ My child does not have permission to ride in a care driven by a volunteer parent

_____
Parent Signature   Date

ITEMS NEEDED FOR THE FIELD TRIP

_____ Signed Permission Slip
_____ Fee ($_____)
_____ Sack Lunch
_____ Extra Clothes
_____ Rubber Boots
_____ Hat
_____ Gloves
_____ Extra Coat

Circle One:
         I WOULD LIKE TO VOLUNTEER TO ASSIST WITH THIS FIELD TRIP
                        YES   NO

PERMISSION TO
TRANSPORT-Limited

I _____ (parent) give permission to

_____ (provider) to transport

_____ (child) in her vehicle, **with**

advance notice, or in the event of an emergency only.

_____

Parent Signature   Date

PERMISSION TO
TRANSPORT

I _____ (parent) give permission to

_____ (provider) to transport

_____ (child) in her vehicle, **at**
anytime.

_____

Parent Signature   Date

EDUCATIONAL PROGRAM PERMISSION SLIP

The undersigned parents, hereby give permission for _____ (child) to participate in the Educational Program, taught by _____ (provider).

We further acknowledge that said Provider is **not** a "certified" instructor, but agree to allow our child to participate and pay additional monthly fee of **$**_____ , for this service.

_____
Parent Signature   Date

EXTRA ACTIVITIES PERMISSION SLIP

The undersigned parents, give permission for _____ (child) to participate in _____ (activity) on _____ , _____. (date), taught by _____ _____ (instructor).

We acknowledge that the person providing this activity is not a licensed child care professional and that there is an additional fee of **$**_____ payable to this person, on or before the date of the scheduled activity.

_____
Parent Signature   Date

Setting Rules for Your Daycare: Your Contract & Policy Handbook

First and foremost, you need to remember, it's your business and it's your home. You are the one who makes the rules and the parents are the ones who agree to follow them. (With the exception of those rules established by your licensing agency.)

Your contract & policies will set the rules for your daycare. Both documents will help create a shared understanding between you & the parents.

What is the difference between a contract and policy?

- Your CONTRACT is a binding legal agreement between two parties. When you make a contract, both parties expect the other to live up to the terms of the agreement. If that promise is broken, either side can seek payment for damages. In the case of a family child care contract, the parties can only seek damages for the failure of the client to pay, or the failure of the provider to deliver child care as stipulated in the contract.

- Your POLICIES are the rules that state in writing how you will care for the children, how you handle specific kids of situations, and how you will run your business. (See enclosed sample).

SUCCESS TIP: Review your entire contract and policy handbook *in person* with EACH set of new parents to your daycare, so they are sure to fully understand the policies and you can then discuss any questions that arise.

Use your licensing agency's rules and the forms enclosed in this book to create the rules for your daycare home.

Begin following your own rules immediately. This will set a precedent for what you will and will not tolerate.

Bending the rules can lead to disaster later on, especially if exceptions are made for some, but not all, of the families enrolled.

Make sure parents know that there will be consequences for breaking the rules. This may include added charges or termination of care. It is imperative that you follow through with these consequences immediately and at all times.

Now it's time to write your contract and policy handbook based on the rules and operation of your daycare.

For a sample contract you can customize to fit your needs, view the Family Child Care Contract found on **pages 58-60.**

Your policy handbook should include how to handle: discipline, behavior, late payments, termination, tardiness, etc.

For an example of a daycare policy handbook, see the sample daycare policy enclosed as a supplement to the Daycare Success System.

Final Thoughts about Contracts & Policies

Being businesslike doesn't mean that you have to be rude or unsympathetic in order to deal successfully with your clients. There is no conflict between being a warm, caring person, and presenting yourself in an organized, businesslike manner.

When negotiating or enforcing a contract with a client, you can be tough without being cold-hearted. Being businesslike simply means sticking to your own rules and setting healthy limits.

It is always appropriate to use assertive behavior to state your policies and enforce your agreements. Although you will not please everyone, most of your clients will come to trust you because you are showing that you have given careful thought to the business of caring for their children.

SUCCESS TIP: Whenever you have an issue with your parent clients, such as a misunderstanding about a certain policy, go back into your Daycare Policy Document and edit that section of the document to make it MORE CLEAR and/or change the policy to fix the problem and ensure that it does not happen again.

Copyright 2008-2013 Daycare Systems LLC

Preparing a Mission Statement

Every business should have a Mission Statement. A mission statement simply spells out what the primary long term goal of the business is. Once charges, fees and services have been determined, it is time to define your mission statement.

As a Daycare Provider, my Mission Statement is:

"To provide a safe and nurturing environment, offer fun activities, nutritious meals and to provide better care than I would expect for my own children"

As the creator of The Daycare Organizer and Attendance Book and the author of The Daycare Provider's Workbook, my Mission Statement is:

"To assist providers in providing quality care, by offering a valuable resource of contacts, activities, and organizational tools, so they can provide better care than they would expect for their own children"

As a Daycare Provider, what will your Mission Statement be?

_____

_____

_____

_____

_____

_____

_____

_____

Use the form on the following page, to post your Mission Statement.

Copyright 2008-2013 Daycare Systems LLC

My Daycare Mission Statement

"
_____

_____

_____

_____

_____

_____
"
_____

Copyright 2008-2013 Daycare Systems LLC

~NOTES~

To get all the forms in this book in an editable form so you can customize them to your daycare visit:

www.DaycareHotline.com/Forms

Copyright 2008-2013 Daycare Systems LLC

Chapter

3

Preparing The Space

Home Preparation

INTERIOR CHECKLIST

Do you have an extra room to use exclusively for the daycare? _____

If you don't have a separate daycare room, where will the children play? _____

Which door will the parents access to drop off and pick up? _____

Where will the Attendance Records be kept, for parents to sign in and out each day? _____

If you use your child's bedroom as the playroom, how will they feel about that? _____

If you are providing an educational program what room would be best for this activity? _____

Where will naps take place, if applicable? _____

Do you have an adequate number of beds, cribs, naps or cots for resting and or napping? _____

If you are caring for infants do you have a sanitary area for changing of diapers? _____

Do you have safety gates that can be put in place while you make a trip to the bathroom or fix a meal? _____

Where will the children place their personal belongings when they arrive? _____

Do you have enough booster seats and high chairs and/or seating for meals? _____

What are the requirements for indoor preparation for your state?

_____

_____

EXTERIOR CHECKLIST

Do you have adequate parking? _____

Do you have a safe entrance to your home? _____
i.e.-railing on stairwells, etc.

Do you have pets? _____ Will they be separated from the
children during hours of operation? _____

Do you have a fenced yard? _____

What outside activities are you able to provide? _____
_____

Do you have cushioning under and surrounding play structures,
to protect against falls? i.e. pea gravel, mats, etc. _____

Will you allow water related activities? _____

If so, what rules and safety precautions have you established for
those activities? _____

Will you allow use of a trampoline during daycare hours?

If you will be monitoring outside play, while infants are napping, do
you have a baby monitor? _____

Can you adequately supervise outdoor activities? _____

Do you have a signed authorization to apply sunscreen? _____

What are the requirements for outdoor safety for your state?
_____

Will your liability insurance protect you in the event a child is injured
while participating in the outdoor activities you offer? _____

Copyright 2008-2013 Daycare Systems LLC

Childproof Checklist

☐ Electrical Outlet covers

☐ Safety Gates

☐ Medications are in childproof containers

☐ Medications are in a cabinet inaccessible to children

☐ Chemicals are out of reach and kept away from food

☐ Only age appropriate toys are within reach

☐ Alcoholic beverages are stored out of reach

☐ Cabinets and drawers are secured with safety latches

☐ Garbage is secured by child proof latches and stored in
a waterproof container with lid

☐ Exterior doors, are childproofed

☐ Mini-blinds and Venetian blinds do not have looped cords

☐ No recalled products in use in your daycare or home

☐ Remove tablecloths or items easily pulled off of furniture or shelves

☐ All indoor and outdoor plants have been confirmed not poisonous

Look around your home. Is there anything else, that needs
to be childproofed?

_____

_____

_____

_____

_____

_____

Copyright 2008-2013 Daycare Systems LLC

State Licensing Home Preparation Checklist

Use this form to compile a list of other State Requirements

- ☐ _____
- ☐ _____
- ☐ _____
- ☐ _____
- ☐ _____
- ☐ _____
- ☐ _____
- ☐ _____
- ☐ _____
- ☐ _____
- ☐ _____
- ☐ _____
- ☐ _____
- ☐ _____
- ☐ _____
- ☐ _____
- ☐ _____
- ☐ _____
- ☐ _____
- ☐ _____
- ☐ _____
- ☐ _____

Copyright 2008-2013 Daycare Systems LLC

Liability Insurance

SUCCESS TIP: It is highly recommended that you purchase Liability Insurance to protect you, your family, your assets and your daycare children.

The cost will be well worth the benefit of the policy, should you ever need to use it.

Liability Insurance can offer you the following protection:

- **DEFENSE COST PROTECTION FROM LAWSUITS**
- **ACCIDENTAL INJURY MEDICAL PAYMENTS**
- **BUSINESS INCOME INTERRUPTION**
- **PROPERTY COVERAGE**
- **PROTECTION FOR INJURIES WHILE ON FIELD TRIPS**

Not all liability insurance policies offer the above protection, shop wisely, when choosing your agent and policy.

Refer to **page 12,** for questions to ask your insurance agent**.**

Let your agent know that you will be operating a daycare in your home. If you are considering purchasing a rider or an endorsement to your existing home owners policy, confirm that you will be covered **for all forms** of damages, listed above and/or any additional coverage you and your agent deem necessary.

As a daycare provider, your business can be affected by liability issues that could arise, in the event that a child is injured while in your care, or your property is damaged.

This coverage can provide you with peace of mind, in the event of a lawsuit or accident.

Liability Insurance may not protect you in the event of an automobile accident. It may only cover "out of car" incidents. Confirm this with your agent, as additional auto insurance coverage may be needed if your are transporting children.

Copyright 2008-2013 Daycare Systems LLC

Setting Up a Daycare Room

A separate room in your home (or separate space such as a finished basement) is ideal but not necessary.

If you do not have a separate room, utilize a corner in your living or family room.

Setting up stations for different activities is great fun for the kids and offers variety when rotated weekly.

Create signs on colored construction paper or poster board and hang them in each station, for the following:

READING/QUIET CORNER
In one corner, place some pillows and a small bookcase, filled with children's books. Encourage the kids to enjoy books, even if they can't read.

MANIPULATIVE
Provide puzzles, blocks, age appropriate games and various manipulative toys on a small table with chairs. If a table and chairs are not available, use an area on the floor.

HOUSEKEEPING
Provide a dress up box with clothes, purses and other accessories. A kid-sized kitchen, if available, would also be a nice addition. Make sure to include pots, pans and pretend food.

CREATION STATION
This area would be for art/projects and learning. Store all art supplies out of reach in large tubs with lids.

FREE PLAY
Provide general toys for unlimited IMAGINATIONS!! Make sure that all the toys available are age appropriate to prevent choking.

REMEMBER, these are just ideas. You can make stations for whatever areas of learning and discovery you choose.

Activities and Toys

For children 2 and under, an appropriate number of the following toys and activities, should be available:

- Board and Picture Books
- Plastic or soft blocks
- Puzzles (simple 2-4 pieces)
- Musical Instruments or Toys
- Push-Pull Toys
- Toys with buttons to push, dials to turn, etc.
- Soft balls
- Art materials-crayons, finger paints– choose these wisely!

For children 2 and older, an appropriate number of the following toys and activities should be available:

- Text books
- Blocks
- Puzzles
- Musical Instruments
- Toys that encourage imagination
- Outdoor equipment
- Paints, crayons, play dough, and other art supplies

Do not keep all the toys available at all times, rotate them weekly. Not only will this reduce the wear and tear on the toys, but will also rejuvenate the interest in toys that are not always available.

Instead of using a toy box, consider sorting toys into clear plastic tubs with lids. Encourage the children to put away the toys they are currently playing with, before moving on to a new toy tub. This should also reduce the search for missing parts and or pieces.

Provide activities that encourage movement and manipulation of objects, for individual use, or use as a group.

A computer is a wonderful educational investment, offering a variety of programs for most age groups.

Copyright 2008-2013 Daycare Systems LLC

Preparing your Family

Before opening your home daycare, sit down with your family and discuss the changes that will be taking place in your home.

Include your family in the decisions you make for your new business.

Below are some helpful hints, to help your kids adjust to your new daycare business:

1) Make your kids a part of creating and planning activities

2) Keep your children's special toys separate from those of the daycare

3) Allow them time alone during the day, in their own room, if they prefer

4) Do not favor your children over the daycare children

5) Do not favor daycare children over your own children

6) If you are using your child's room as part of the daycare, make it a rule, that the kids have to clean the room up, every night before they go home

7) Give your kids some special time after all the kids leave for the day, just to cuddle, read a book or talk

8) Talk to your kids, encourage them to discuss any issues that arise about daycare, daycare children or about sharing you

9) Screen your families carefully, including the children and do not allow bullies or destructive children into your home daycare

10) Operating a home business, can be chaotic at times. You will need the support of both your family and spouse. Prepare them, so they will be available when you look to them for guidance or support.

 Copyright 2008-2013 Daycare Systems LLC

~Notes~

Sign up for weekly educational training from the Daycare Success Coach Kris Murray at
www.DaycareHotline.com

Copyright 2008-2013 Daycare Systems LLC

Marketing & Advertising

Copyright 2008-2013 Daycare Systems LLC

Free Advertising Ideas

Before spending any money on advertising, use the following contacts as a starting point.

- Contact all Elementary Schools on your bus line or in your area. Most schools maintain a list of Childcare Providers, which they provide to parents upon request. Ask to have your name and phone number added to their Provider list.

- Contact Your Local Branch of the Child Care Resource & Referral Agency. This is the very first thing you should do to get your name out there, and it should be done prior to opening your doors. The website is located at: http://www.childcareaware.org. Then enter your ZIP Code in the search field and you will receive the contact information for your nearest CCR&R. You can also call them toll-free at (800) 424-2246. Once you register, they will provide your contact information, along with any special information pertaining to your daycare, to parents seeking child care.

  As of December 2007, in order to be registered with CCR&R, you do not need to be state-licensed or certified. However, they request that solo family daycare providers have a maximum of 6 children at any time, and no more than 3 children under the age of 2. If there is more than one caregiver in the home/facility, the numbers can be higher. These numbers vary by state, so be sure to call your local CCR&R branch to confirm these rules.

- Enroll in a Food Program, they too will provide your name and number to parents seeking childcare.

- Tell everyone you know that you are providing Childcare and ask them if they know anyone who is seeking childcare in your area. This may be your strongest source for enrolling daycare children. Most parents prefer to leave their children with a provider that was recommended by a friend, neighbor, coworker or family member.

- Ask an organization you belong to such as a Church, or Play group, if you can place an announcement in their Newsletter. If you know a business professional that mails out a newsletter, ask them to advertise your business for the local residents on their database.

- Introduce yourself to existing providers in your area. They may be willing to refer parents to you, in the event their daycare is full or they leave the industry.

- List your program on Craigslist (www.Craigslist.org). This is one of the most successful methods for filling your program. There is a special section for Child Care. Research Craigslist ads from other providers and model the ones you find most appealing.

Low Cost Advertising Ideas

- Create a flyer and distribute it to businesses in your area: Real Estate Offices, Banks, Grocery Stores, and Professional Offices.

- Post flyers on Bulletin Boards at the Grocery Store, Post Office, etc.

- Place a small ad in your local paper, or in the service directory.

- Create an announcement letter, similar to the one on **page 49.**

- Mail the announcement letter to everyone on your list If they do not need daycare, ask them to pass it on to someone who does, or to post it in there place of business when applicable.

- If you are offering specialized care, such as 24 hour, weekend or evening only care, seek out those companies that work split or odd shifts to advertise your daycare.

- For more great strategies and tips on building enrollment and promoting your program, visit the author at www.childcare-marketing.com

Busy Hands Daycare

West Linn Willamette area Home Daycare has openings for your children ages 6 months to 6 years.

Our Program Consists of:
Daily Schedule
Age appropriate activities
Nutritious Meals and Snacks
Safe and Nurturing Environment
Ratios of 1-4
State Registered
Infant Child CPR Certified
Large Fenced Back Yard
Limited TV viewing
Computer Activities

Busy Hands Daycare
Jane
123-4567

Busy Hands Daycare
Jane
123-4567

Busy Hands Daycare
Jane
123-4567

Busy Hands Daycare
Jane
123-4567

Busy Hands Daycare
Jane
123-4567

Busy Hands Daycare
Jane
123-4567

Busy Hands Daycare
Jane
123-4567

Busy Hands Daycare
Jane
123-4567

Copyright 2008-2013 Daycare Systems LLC

ANNOUNCING............

The opening of:
Busy Hands Daycare

I am proud to announce that I have recently opened my Home Daycare.

I'm very excited about this venture and have registered with the State, participate in the USDA Food Program, received CPR/First Aid Training and belong to my local Childcare Resource and Referral Agency.

I only have a few openings and would appreciate you passing this announcement letter to someone who may be seeking QUALITY Childcare.

Thank you in advance for your support. I look forward to hearing from you.

Jane Smith
Busy Hands Daycare
Anywhere, USA
503-123-4567

Copyright 2008-2013 Daycare Systems LLC

NAME:
ADDRESS:
PHONE:

NAME:
ADDRESS:
PHONE:

NAME:
ADDRESS:
PHONE:

NAME:
ADDRESS:
PHONE:

NAME:
ADDRESS:
PHONE:

NAME:
ADDRESS:
PHONE:

NAME:
ADDRESS:
PHONE:

NAME:
ADDRESS:
PHONE:

NAME:
ADDRESS:
PHONE:

NAME:
ADDRESS:
PHONE:

NAME:
ADDRESS:
PHONE:

NAME:
ADDRESS:
PHONE:

NAME:
ADDRESS:
PHONE:

NAME:
ADDRESS:
PHONE:

NAME:
ADDRESS:
PHONE:

NAME:
ADDRESS:
PHONE:

NAME:
ADDRESS:
PHONE:

NAME:
ADDRESS:
PHONE:

Copyright 2008-2013 Daycare Systems LLC

Interviews and Enrollment Forms

Conducting Parent Interviews

Keep in mind, that not only are you being interviewed, but you are interviewing the parents. If at anytime during the interview process you become uncomfortable, then refuse to provide care. It will be very tempting, especially when you are first opening your doors, to take every child that needs care. Unfortunately, you will not be able to provide care for everyone that calls, or for everyone that you interview.

Step 1

Always phone interview parents first, using the Phone Interview Checklist. This should give you an idea of what they are looking for in a daycare provider and if you will be able to meet their needs. This will also provide you with information about the parents before you invite them into your home.

Step 2

Complete the Phone Interview Check list, do not hesitate to ask any questions you feel may apply during the conversation.

There is more to providing Quality care than how much you charge. For example, the number of children you care for, what type of program you offer and if you have CPR/First Aid Certification. If a parent's primary concern is the amount you charge for childcare, then proceed with caution!

This example, is just one of many "red flags" that you will need to watch for during the phone and face to face interview. Another example, are those parents who want to negotiate your fees, change your pay dates, or policies in your contract.

If parents want to tell you how to operate your business before you start providing care, how will they be to work with during the course of caring for their children?

Don't hesitate to ask for references, especially if they are changing providers. Find out why? Call the provider and see if you get the same answer from her, as provided by the parent.

 Copyright 2008-2013 Daycare Systems LLC

Step 3

If you feel comfortable with the Phone Interview, set up a time for the parents to interview in your home, during your hours of operation.
Let the parents know ahead of time, that the interview needs to last no more than 30 minutes, so you can tend to the needs of your other day-care children. They can always return for a second visit, if necessary.

Step 4

Notify existing daycare parents of potential interviews. As a safety pre-caution, consider letting a neighbor, friend or relative know that you will be interviewing someone that you do not know. Provide them with the parents name, number, what time the interview will take place and ask them to call you sometime during the interview.

Step 5

Have all forms available at the Interview for review and signatures if needed.

The Interview Checklist is located on the next page.

Interview Checklist

Ask the following questions, before setting up the "in-home" interview. Keep in mind, this is your business, you do not have to provide care for anyone that makes you feel uncomfortable.

What type of care are you looking for? _____

What hours and days do you need care? _____

How many children do you have? _____

What are their names and ages? _____

_____

Is he/she potty trained? _____

Does he/she take a bottle? _____

Where do you work and live? _____

Have your children had prior daycare experiences? _____

Were they in-home or facility care situations? _____

Why are you changing providers? _____

When do you need daycare to begin? _____

When would you like to set up an Interview? _____

What is your name and phone number? _____

_____

Interview Date and Time: _____

Copyright 2008-2013 Daycare Systems LLC

The Face to Face Interview

Be professional, neat and organized, this will not only help your interview run smoothly, it will also help your business run smoothly.

- Use the Phone Interview Checklist to confirm the information you obtained during the phone interview.

- Explain your daily schedule and activities

- Review your rules and discipline policies

- Show parents where they will sign in and out each day

- Inform families if you plan on having parties on holidays and birth-days. Some families may not want their children to participate in these activities for various reasons.

- Discuss your Contract, Enrollment, Authorization Forms and any other forms, you want signed at Enrollment Time

- Provide your Policy Handbook to the parent(s) and ask them to read through it in the next few days, then get back to you with any questions.

- If you participate in a Food Program, explain the program and have any necessary forms signed.

- Explain your rates, and payment dates. Also inform them of the days your daycare will be closed, throughout the year.

- At the end of the Interview, offer a "tour" of your home and yard. Show parents where their children will play, eat, use the bathroom and where diaper changes will take place.

If at the end of the interview, you choose to provide care for the child, offer a one or two hour visit, without the parents. This will give you a better idea of what the child/ren are actually like. An authorization form for this visit is located at the back of this section.

If you accept the child, you can then schedule a 30-minute meeting with the parents to sit down and review the Policy Handbook with them.

CHILDCARE ENROLLMENT
INFORMATION & AUTHORIZATION FORM
(One form must be completed for each child in care)

Name of Provider: _____
Date of entry: _____ Child's age & Birth date: _____
Child's full Name: _____

PARENTS CAN BE REACHED:

Name: _____Relationship: _____
Home Phone Number: _____ Cell/Pager: _____
Home Address: _____
Employer Name: _____ Phone: _____
Address: _____ Hours: _____

Name: _____ Relationship: _____
Home Phone Number: _____ Cell/Pager: _____
Home Address: _____
Employer Name: _____ Phone: _____
Address: _____ Hours: _____

IF PARENTS OR GUARDIANS CANNOT BE REACHED CONTACT:

Name: _____ Relationship: _____
Address: _____ Phone: _____

Child's Doctor: _____ Phone: _____
Address:_____
Child's Dentist: _____ Phone: _____
Address:_____
What hospital do you prefer: _____
Name of Child's School: _____ Phone: _____

Who besides you is authorized to pick up children: *
Name: _____ Phone: _____
Relationship to child: _____
Name: _____ Phone: _____
Relationship to child: _____

*Identification will be required by these individuals, in the event they pick up your child.

www.DaycareHotline.com   Copyright 2008-2013 Daycare Systems LLC

PERMISSION IS GIVEN TO CHILDCARE PROVIDER FOR THE FOLLOWING:
A check indicates approval

_____ In an emergency, the above named provider has my permission to call an ambulance or to take my child to any available physician or hospital at my expense.

_____ In an emergency, the above named provider has my permission to obtain medical treatment for my child, except these restrictions, if any

_____

ADDITIONAL INFORMATION:

Eating habits & schedule: _____

Sleeping schedule: _____

Fears: _____

Likes and Dislikes: _____

Special words and their meanings:

_____

Has your child every had Chicken Pox?   YES   NO

Does your child have any Allergies?   YES   NO

If yes, please explain: _____

_____

Does your child have any health problems that restrict their activities? YES   NO

If yes, please explain: _____

_____

Has your child been immunized?   YES   NO

PLEASE ATTACH A COPY OF UP TO DATE IMMUNIZATION RECORDS

_____   _____

Parent Signature   Date

_____   _____

Parent Signature   Date

FAMILY CHILD CARE CONTRACT

Payment in the amount of _____ per day/week/hour (circle one) per child
is payable to: _____ **(PROVIDER)** for childcare provided per
childcare schedule below and the attached payment option.

CHILD CARE SCHEDULE:
(Circle Days that care is needed) Monday Tuesday Wednesday Thursday Friday
(Complete Hours) Care is needed _____ a.m./p.m. to _____ a.m./p.m.
Other: _____

PAYMENT IS DUE: _____ **with no exceptions.**

LATE FEES AND NSF FEES:
$_____ **late fee** for each day that payment is **overdue.**
Care will not be available, until payment is made in full.
$_____ **returned check fee.** Any returned checks, will result in future
payments of cash only. The amount of the returned check plus the fee, is due
immediately to provider.
$_____ **per minute,** if care is provided after _____ p.m. or after _____ hours.

SICK DAYS:
Childcare will not be available for children exhibiting more than minor cold symptoms,
which impair their functioning. Parents agree to pick up children within _____ hours of
notification, should their child become ill.

ILLNESS:
All communicable illnesses will be reported to parents immediately.

ABSENCES:
See payment plan for charges.

VACATIONS:
Two weeks notice required, prior to absence. See payment plan for charges.

HOLIDAYS AND CLOSURES:
Our home Daycare is closed on the following days:

_____
_____
_____
_____

Other closures may occur due to provider illness, family emergencies and medical or
doctor appointments, provider will give notice of closures as soon as available.

BACK UP CARE:
Is not provided by the Daycare Provider. It is the sole responsibility of the parent to obtain back up care.

DISCIPLINE:
All discipline will be handled according to age.
For Toddlers and Infants, redirection will be implemented.
For Preschool and School Age children, time outs will be given after two verbal warnings and redirection.

BEHAVIOR:
The undersigned parents acknowledge that should their child exhibit aggressive behavior or behavior that the provider deems uncontrollable or excessive, they will be contacted by the provider and asked to pick up their child/ren immediately.

TRIAL BASIS:
All parties agree and acknowledge that the first 2 weeks of care is provided on a temporary basis.

TERMINATION:
All parties agree and acknowledge that either party will be required to give 2 weeks notice, prior to termination of care and/or services. Upon notice of termination, payment is due in full.

RATE INCREASES:
Provider reserves the right to increase childcare rates at the end of each year, at an increase of _____ per day, week or hour, with 30 days written notice.

AGREEMENT:
I agree to follow the guidelines set forth in this contract and to pay the fees as stated. I understand that if the above guidelines are not followed, the provider has the right to refuse service and/or terminate the agreement to provide care.

DATE CARE IS TO BEGIN: _____

_____   _____
Parent Signature   Date   Provider Signature   Date

Address: _____   Address: _____

_____   _____

Phone: _____   Phone: _____

WEEKLY PAYMENT OPTION

$_____ per week, per child, for _____ weeks per year. This amount is to be paid even if my children are not in the providers care.

DAILY PAYMENT OPTION

$_____ per day, per child. I agree to pay for a minimum of _____days per week. This amount is to be paid even if my children is not in the providers care.

SICK DAYS AND ABSENCES:
I understand that I will not be charged when my child is sick or absent, as long as I contact the provider within 1 hour of normal drop off time. I will be allowed a maximum of _____ sick days per year, without charge. I (parent) agree to pay for additional sick days at the rate of $_____ per day missed.
I understand that I will not be charged when my child is absent, as long as I contact the provider within 1 hour of normal drop off time. In the event the provider is not contacted, I agree to pay a charge of $_____.

VACATIONS:
I (parent) acknowledge and agree to pay an additional charge of $_____ per week, in the event that vacations exceed 2 weeks per year.

HOURLY PAYMENT OPTION

$_____ per hour, per child.

I understand that I will not be charged when my child is absent, as long as I contact the provider within 1 hour of normal drop off time. In the event the provider is not contacted, I agree to pay a charge of $_____.

_____   _____
Parent   Date   Provider   Date

PERMISSION TO APPLY SUNSCREEN

I _____ (parent), give permission to

_____ (provider) to apply sunscreen I have

provided for _____ (child) beginning on

_____ (date) until _____ (date).

_____
Parent Signature   Date

PRE-CARE VISIT AUTHORIZATION

The undersigned parents agree to allow _____ (child)
to visit _____ (daycare)
on _____ (date) from _____ to _____ (time).

The parents further acknowledge that this visit is not an agreement to provide childcare.

Emergency Contact Information:

Name: _____   Phone: _____

_____
Parent Signature   Date

Copyright 2008-2013 Daycare Systems LLC

~NOTES~

To get all the forms in this book in an editable form so you can customize them to your daycare visit:

www.DaycareHotline.com/Forms

Copyright 2008-2013 Daycare Systems LLC

Health and Safety

Copyright 2008-2013 Daycare Systems LLC

Illnesses and Infections

Each state has different guidelines in regards to caring for children with certain illnesses, infections or diseases. Review your states policy on caring for sick children prior to allowing them into your daycare home.

If after reviewing your state's policy you have questions, contact the licensing agency, local health department or your pediatrician for more information. Contact your local resource and referral agency for available courses, covering this topic.

If a child arrives at your daycare with obvious symptoms, do not allow the parent to leave the child in your care.

When children become ill while in your care, contact parents and isolate the child from the other children, until the parents arrive.

Notify all other parents, when sending a child home ill, so they can watch for symptoms in their children.

Enforce your illness policy without fail. Parents who bring their children to daycare, knowing they are ill, should be reminded of your rules on this matter and termination should be enforced, if necessary.

Disinfect your home and bathrooms daily, and immediately after sending children home ill.

Keep diaper changing area near a sink. Use disposable changing pads and wipe down the changing table with an antibacterial cleaner after each use. Wear disposable gloves for every diaper change, changing gloves and washing hands between children. Have each family provide its own container of baby wipes, labeled with their infants name.

Make hand washing a regular activity for all children and yourself throughout the day.
- Before and after eating
- After using the bathroom
- After blowing noses
- After diaper changes-even if using disposable gloves

Administering Medications

Prior to administering medication, have parents complete and sign an authorization form. This form should be used each time medication is administered, even for non prescription drugs.

Any medications administered, should be provided by the parents in it's original container and labeled with the child's name, the amount of medication to be given and when.

Carefully read the label to ensure you are giving the proper dosage and properly storing the medication. As the medication is administered, a written record of the disbursements should be recorded and kept in the child's file.

Provide a copy of the completed form to the parents, along with the remaining medication.

As with all medications, keep out of the reach of children.

Note: Before allowing children who are on medication into your daycare home, confirm the nature of the illness and that they are beyond the contagious stage, or ask for a doctor's note.

An authorization for administration of medication is on the following page.

Check with your state licensing agency to see if they have additional rules and regulations regarding the administration of medication.

Note: Another option is for you to have a policy that requires all medications to be administered by parents or others. Many child care centers have this policy to protect themselves from liability.

Copyright 2008-2013 Daycare Systems LLC

PERMISSION TO ADMINISTER MEDICATION

I _____(parent) give permission to

_____(provider) to administer the following

medication _____

to _____(child).

Beginning on _____ until _____.

_____
Parent   (date)

I _____(provider) administered the above
medication as follows:

Date: _____   Time: _____   Amount: _____

Date: _____   Time: _____   Amount: _____

Date: _____   Time: _____   Amount: _____

Date: _____   Time: _____   Amount: _____

Date: _____   Time: _____   Amount: _____

On _____ (date) remaining medication was returned to the above
parent.

_____
Provider Signature   Date

Parent acknowledges the return of the medication and a copy of this form

_____
Parent Signature   Date

Cleaning Checklist

Disinfect after each use:

- ☐ Diaper Changing area
- ☐ Training Seats and Toilets
- ☐ Cooking area

At the end of each day:

- ☐ Sweep, mop and disinfect kitchen counter and floors
- ☐ Sweep, mop and disinfect bathroom counter and floors
- ☐ Disinfect Diaper Change Area
- ☐ Vacuum carpets
- ☐ Wipe down Cribs and/or Playpens
- ☐ Air out your home for approximately 15 minutes

At the end of each week:

- ☐ Mop Floors, primarily Kitchen and Bathrooms
- ☐ Disinfect all mouth-able toys
- ☐ Disinfect Bathrooms
- ☐ Disinfect Kitchens
- ☐ Disinfect Diaper Changing Area
- ☐ Vacuum
- ☐ Wipe down Cribs and/or Playpens
- ☐ Wash Bedding

At the end of each month:

- ☐ Wipe down all toys
- ☐ Deep Clean entire home, especially primary daycare area

Injury

If Infant-Child CPR and First Aid Certification is not required by your state licensing agency, take the initiative to obtain this certification.

Every daycare home and vehicle should have an easily accessible, First Aid Kit, which should contain the following:

- Disposable gloves
- Alcohol wipes or antiseptic wipes
- Scissors
- Tweezers
- Thermometer
- Adhesive Tape
- Sterile gauze squares
- Band Aids of all sizes
- Flexible roller gauze
- Eye Dressing
- Insect Sting ointment
- Pencil and Paper
- Ipecac Syrup
- Cold Pack
- Small splints
- Seal-able plastic bags (for soiled materials)
- First Aid Guide

In addition to your First Aid Kit, also keep ice bags or cold packs on hand.

If a child is injured, apply the appropriate First Aid and complete an accident report, which should be given to the parent when they pick up their child. Retain a copy of the report for your records.

Check your Licensing rules and regulations for proper procedures, if any, on reporting injuries to the agency.

In the event of a serious injury, DO NOT PANIC! Call 911 and contact the parents immediately.

ACCIDENT

Copyright 2008-2013 Daycare Systems LLC

REPORT

On _____ (date) _____ (child)

was injured when _____

_____ the provider

APPLIED THE FOLLOWING:
(Only circled items apply)
ICE   BAND-AID HUG
Called parent   YES   NO
Called for medical attention YES   NO
Comments:

_____

_____

ACCIDENT
REPORT

On _____ (date) _____ (child)

was injured when _____

_____the provider

APPLIED THE FOLLOWING:
(Only circled items apply)
ICE   BAND-AID HUG
Called parent   YES   NO
Called for medical attention YES   NO
Comments:

_____

_____

Abuse

If training on how to recognize and report Child Abuse, is not required, you should seek such training. Child abuse can be emotional, verbal, physical, sexual or caused by neglect.

Possible signs of abuse include:
Physical Abuse
Injuries in the shape of an object
Repetitious or unexplained bruises, welts or burns
Obvious neglect of a child

Emotional/Verbal Abuse
Fear of going home
Excessive behavior-aggressive or withdrawal
Avoidance of physical contact with parents or adults

Sexual Abuse
Child verbally tells you he/she was sexually mistreated
Stained or bloody underwear
Genital or Rectal pain and/or bruising in those areas
Difficulty eating or sleeping
Excessive crying or sadness
Talking about or acting out sexual acts

If you suspect a child is being abused:
- Record all suspicions, times and dates
- Maintain these records in the child's file
- Contact the authorities in your area responsible for Child Abuse Reporting
- Keep a record of the calls you place to the authorities and the conversations that take place

When in doubt, or if you would like more information, contact the Child Abuse Center for your state, these numbers are located in **Appendix C.**

As a provider you will be required by law to report child abuse.

Safety

As a childcare Provider, you will be responsible for the safety and well being of the children in your care.

As mentioned earlier in this book, you should provide a safe environment for all age groups. This can be accomplished by the following:

- ☐ Well supervised indoor and outdoor play
- ☐ Childproof your Home
- ☐ Do not allow strangers into your home during business hours
- ☐ Maintain daily logs of attendance and only release children to authorized individuals
- ☐ Keep your home clean and well ventilated
- ☐ Install the appropriate numbers of smoke detectors and fire extinguishers (see your states rules for specifics)
- ☐ Check smoke detectors monthly (log on calendar)
- ☐ Maintaining a well equipped First Aid Kit
- ☐ Set Hot Water Heater thermostat at 120 degrees
- ☐ Post emergency numbers by each phone (use the form on **page 73** copy onto heavy paper and laminate)
- ☐ Create a Power Outage Plan
- ☐ Flashlights or back up light source are available throughout home
- ☐ Prepare and Post in a visible location Fire Evacuation and Disaster Plans. Practice these plans on a monthly basis.
- ☐ Use the form on **page 72** to sketch your floor plan. Draw each level of your home. Show two exits from each room. Choose a safe meeting place outside. Complete emergency phone numbers and information.
- ☐ Monthly Fire Drills (log this on your calendar)
- ☐ Prepare and post disaster plans in areas of Tornadoes, Hurricanes, Earthquakes and other natural disasters. For tips on these plans, contact your state emergency services or licensing agency.

Copyright 2008-2013 Daycare Systems LLC

Fire Escape Plan

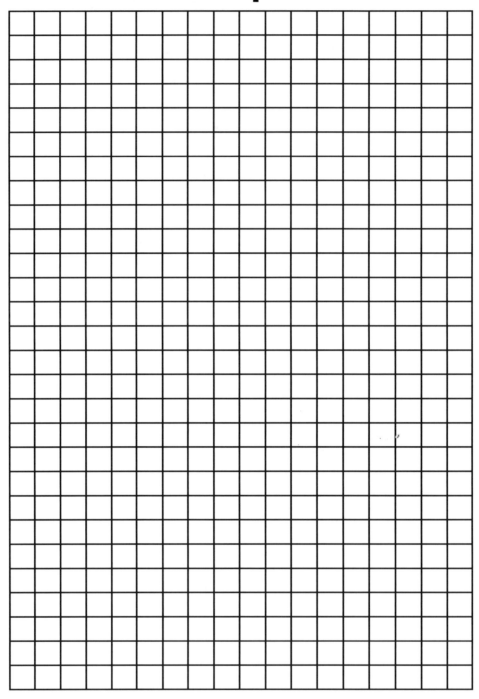

Call: <u>911</u> Fire Dept.: _____
Address: _____

Copyright 2008-2013 Daycare Systems LLC

EMERGENCY NUMBERS
911

Fire Dept: _____ **Police:** _____

Poison Control: _____

Child Abuse Hotline: _____

State Licensing Agency: _____

Your Address: _____

Cross Street: _____

Child's Name: _____ **DOB:** _____

Allergies: _____

Parents Names/Numbers: Home: _____

Mom Work: _____ **Dad Work:** _____

Physician: _____ **Number:** _____

Child's Name: _____ **DOB:** _____

Allergies: _____

Parents Names/Numbers: Home: _____

Mom Work: _____ **Dad Work:** _____

Physician: _____ **Number:** _____

Child's Name: _____ **DOB:** _____

Allergies: _____

Parents Names/Numbers: Home: _____

Mom Work: _____ **Dad Work:** _____

Physician: _____ **Number:** _____

Copyright 2008-2013 Daycare Systems LLC

~NOTES~

Get the 2 Hour Audio Companion to this workbook and hear from the author even more great information:
www.DaycareHotline.com/Audio

Copyright 2008-2013 Daycare Systems LLC

Meal Planning

Copyright 2008-2013 Daycare Systems LLC

Meal Planning

The expense and time involved in preparing meals can be costly.
The following tips may help in reducing your time and money spent.

Buy in Bulk

Crackers, canned fruits and vegetables, pasta, rice and other foods
used on a regular basis, should be purchased in large quantities. A
membership at a "warehouse style" grocer may be well worth the
cost of the annual fee to purchase foods and household supplies in bulk.

Make ahead and freeze

Many meals can be made ahead, frozen and reheated at a later date,
such as: Beef Stew or Lasagna.

Plan Ahead

Before shopping, plan out the snacks and meals you plan to prepare
for the week. Forms for weekly planning are on **pages 79-81.**

Double It**

Plan your meals and snacks to coincide with your family meals.
For example, if you are serving your family the following for dinner:
Monday-Spaghetti
Tuesday-Chicken and Rice
Wednesday-Tacos
Thursday-Tuna Casserole
Double the amount you are preparing for your family's meal and
serve it for lunch the following day.
Any left over food, should be covered, labeled, refrigerated and used
within 36 hours, or frozen immediately.

Keep the grocery list available, to avoid running out of staples, such as
milk, cheese, eggs, bread, fruits and vegetables.

**If using this tip, make sure that your Food Program, does not require
that your daycare food be kept separate from your family's food!

Food Handling Safety

If a Food Handler's card is not a state requirement, consider reading a Food Handler's Manual, or obtaining a Food Handler's Card which will contain important information regarding safe food handling.

The following are tips on Safe Food Handling:

Wash your hands before:
- Touching anything used to prepare food
- Handling foods that will not be cooked
- Eating

Wash your hands after:
- Touching raw poultry, fish or meats
- Handling trash or dirty dishes
- Eating or going to the bathroom
- Blowing your nose, coughing or sneezing

Use a thermometer when cooking meats and or poultry.

Never allow cooked foods to sit at room temperature for more than 30 minutes. Thaw frozen foods in the refrigerator, under cool running water or in a microwave oven. Once thawed, cook and serve immediately.

Nutrition and Food Programs

Refer to the **page 10**, for questions to ask your local Food Program Sponsor.

A Food Program Sponsor can provide you with valuable information regarding nutrition, recipes and snack ideas.

Should you decide not to become a participant, it may be worth while, to take a class or obtain information on Nutrition and/or serving healthy well balanced meals and snacks.

Kitchen Tips

- Select scheduled times for meals and snacks

- Plan your snacks or meals ahead of time

- Serve easy to fix meals and snacks to reduce cooking times

- Hand washing should be completed prior to preparing any meal or snack

- Have all children seated in an eating area for meals and snacks

- Do not allow children to walk around with food, bottles or cups

- Serve only 100% fruit juice, be sure to read the label for ingredients, before purchasing

- Serve juice sparingly, too much juice can be attributed to poor eating habits, when children are too full of juice to eat the appropriate amount of food

- Serve fats, candy, soda and high sugar foods sparingly

- Encourage good eating habits, by serving and eating nutritious foods

- Don't force children to eat

- Repetition is the key to getting children to eat vegetables and fruits

- Encourage use of utensils and napkins

- Hand washing should be completed before and after each meal or snack

- Clean kitchen during and after meals or snacks

Copyright 2008-2013 Daycare Systems LLC

5 Day Weekly Meal Planner

	MONDAY	TUESDAY	WEDNESDAY	THURSDAY	FRIDAY
BREAKFAST					
SNACK					
LUNCH					
SNACK					
DINNER					

www.DaycareHotline.com   Copyright 2008-2013 Daycare Systems LLC

5 Day Weekly Meal Planner

	MONDAY	TUESDAY	WEDNESDAY	THURSDAY	FRIDAY
BREAKFAST					
SNACK					
LUNCH					
SNACK					

Copyright 2008-2013 Daycare Systems LLC

7 Day Weekly Meal Planner

	SUNDAY	MONDAY	TUESDAY	WEDNESDAY	THURSDAY	FRIDAY	SATURDAY
BREAKFAST							
SNACK							
LUNCH							
SNACK							
DINNER							

Copyright 2008-2013 Daycare Systems LLC

Grocery List

DAIRY
- MILK
- EGGS
- CHEESE
- COTTAGE CHEESE
- BUTTER
- MARGARINE
- SOUR CREAM
- YOGURT
- CREAM
- CREAM CHEESE

MEATS
- PIZZA
- LUNCH MEAT
- STEW MEAT
- HOT DOGS
- SAUSAGE
- PORK CHOPS
- HAMBURGER
- RIBS
- BACON
- CHICKEN
- FISH
- STEAK

SNACK ITEMS
- GRANOLA BARS
- PRETZELS
- CHIPS
- PICKLES
- COOKIES
- RICE CAKES
- CRACKERS

PRODUCE
- APPLES
- BANANAS
- ORANGES
- APRICOTS
- PEACHES
- PLUMS
- NECTARINES
- GRAPEFRUIT
- GRAPES
- PEARS
- CANTALOUPE
- WATERMELON
- HONEY DEW
- PEAS
- CARROTS
- BROCCOLI
- ASPARAGUS
- CORN
- BEANS
- CAULIFLOWER
- POTATOES
- PEPPERS
- LETTUCE
- AVOCADO
- TOMATOES
- SPROUTS
- ONIONS
- MUSHROOMS
- CUCUMBERS

BAKING
- FLOUR
- SUGAR
- SALT
- BAKING POWDER OR SODA
- SHORTENING
- NUTS
- CAKE MIX
- FROSTING
- CHOCOLATE CHIPS
- RAISINS

BREADS/CEREALS PASTAS
- CEREAL
- OATMEAL
- BREAD
- BAGELS
- RICE
- MUFFINS
- MACARONI & CHEESE
- PASTA
- SPAGHETTI
- LASAGNA
- TACO SHELLS
- TORTILLAS

SPREADS/SAUCES
- PEANUT BUTTER
- JAM
- SPAGHETTI SAUCE
- SALSA
- TACO SAUCE
- SOY SAUCE
- MAYONNAISE
- MUSTARD

SEASONINGS
- KETCHUP
- OIL
- SYRUP
- HONEY
- LEMON JUICE
- BROTH
- ENCHILADA SAUCE

BEVERAGES
- JUICE
- POP
- COFFEE
- TEA
- KOOL-AID
- WATER

FROZEN FOODS
- ICE CREAM
- POPCICLES
- WAFFLES
- JUICE
- PIZZA
- VEGETABLES
- BREAD DOUGH
- DESSERTS
- FROZEN ENTREES

CANNED FOODS
- CHILI
- SOUPS
- STEW
- VEGETABLES
- FRUITS
- REFRIED BEANS
- TOMATOES
- BROTH
- ENCHILADA SAUCE

MISC.

CLEANING SUPPLIES
- LAUNDRY DETERGENT
- FABRIC SOFTENER
- BLEACH
- DISH SOAP
- HAND SOAP
- DISHWASHER DETERGENT
- BAR SOAP
- FLOOR CLEANER
- BATH AND BOWL CLEANERS
- FURNITURE POLISH
- TOILET PAPER
- NAPKINS
- PAPER TOWELS

Copyright 2008-2013 Daycare Systems LLC

Snack Ideas and Recipes

Snacks should include at least two of the following: milk or milk product, fruit, vegetable, peanut butter, whole grain or enriched bread, cereal or crackers, 100 percent fruit juice.

Crackers and Cheese
Juice and Crackers
Cheese and Fruit
Trail Mix and Juice
Bagels with Cheese
Raisins or Dried Fruit and Milk
Celery sticks w/Peanut Butter and Milk
Carrot sticks and Juice
Homemade Cookies and Milk
Granola Bars and Milk
Peanut Butter Roll Ups and Milk

Peanut Butter Roll Ups
Warm Soft Flour Tortillas for 30 seconds in microwave.
Spread each with peanut butter.
Roll, cut in half and serve.

Ants on a Log
Spread peanut butter on celery sticks and top with raisins

Trail Mix
1 cup cheese crackers, 1 cup pretzel twists, 1 cup raisins

Cheese Sticks
Take one loaf of frozen bread dough and thaw in greased pan for
2-4 hours. Divide dough into 8-10 sections. Brush with melted butter.
Roll in grated parmesan cheese and sprinkle with grated cheddar cheese.
Bake at 350 degrees until golden brown, approximately 20 minutes.

Copyright 2008-2013 Daycare Systems LLC

~Notes~

Sign up for weekly educational training from the Daycare Success Coach Kris Murray at
www.DaycareHotline.com

Copyright 2008-2013 Daycare Systems LLC

Infants and Toddlers

Copyright 2008-2013 Daycare Systems LLC

Infants and Toddlers

When dealing with infants and toddlers, remember that you will need to cater to their schedules and needs. If you want to specialize, make sure you don't take more children than you can provide QUALITY care for.

Your state will have regulations as to the number of children you can care for in different age categories. Prior to caring for infants and toddlers, review your states rules and regulations, so you will be in compliance.

Completing the "Look What I did to day Sheet" on a daily basis, will keep parents informed of their children's daily activities and your need for supplies. Two versions of this form are on **pages 90 and 91.**

Infant and Toddler Checklist

_____ Home has been Childproofed, see the Childproof Checklist on **page 38**

_____ Sufficient bedding/cribs and playpens are available for nap time

_____ Toys are age appropriate and mouthable

_____ Safety gates are in place

_____ Rates have been established for children not potty trained

_____ Appropriate number of high chairs, booster seats, and childproof eating utensils are available

_____ It has been determined who is to provide formula, the parents or the provider

_____ Attend Early Childhood Development courses.

 Copyright 2008-2013 Daycare Systems LLC

Through play, children learn:

- Social Skills
- Visual Stimulation Fine Motor skills (crafts/baking/scissors)
- Spatial Relationships (top to bottom/in to out)
- Gross Motor Skills (sitting/walking)
- Hand Eye Coordination (fitting shapes)
- Cognitive Skills (enhances imagination and concentration)
- Communication (ability to play out real life roles, process thinking and/or feelings)

The main ingredient for Infants and Toddlers should be PLAY!

Play offers:
- Open ended explorations
- Power and Self Direction
- Through total absorption they work out problems, make choices and find out what interests them
- Early play is an important foundation for later learning and understanding

An adults role in play:
- Allow children to resolve conflicts, as long as it is playful
- Engage in mutual play, but don't direct
- Provide safety and help with problem solving

What an individual can learn and how he learns it, depends on what model he or she has available

Young Infants	Mobile Infants	Toddler
Security	Exploration	Identity
Trust	Adventure	Self
Closeness	Discovery	Their surroundings
Safe	Growth	Impact
Love	Curiosity	Anatomy
Free	Freedom	Power

- Children can learn through Praise, Attention, Feedback and Modeling
- **Be a great model for learning!!!**

Infants and Toddlers are at different levels of development and need different things from their providers.

What can you do as a provider to facilitate those needs?

Copyright 2008-2013 Daycare Systems LLC

Environment

One's physical environment has an impact on learning. As a provider your environment should: promote health, comfort, convenience, be child friendly/sized, offer flexibility and safety, offer choices, and encourage movement.

What can you do as a provider to offer this environment?

Remember the following, can assist you in providing a safe and nurturing environment for Infants and Toddlers:

- **Don't push** babies into positions they can't get into themselves. Babies get themselves ready for standing by sitting & crawling, **not by being stood up**

- **Don't teach** Gross Motor Skills
  Encourage practice of what they know how to do.

- **Muscles Develop**
  Head > Shoulders > Trunk
  Sit > Roll > Crawl > Walk

- **Stability** is the means to **mobility**

- **Toddlers need freedom** to move and experience in a variety of ways using what they have-carrying, dumping, music, movement, dance

- Be **responsive** to the needs of each individual child

- Allow **self-directe**d Free Play

- **Keep group size small**

- **Observe don't interfere**

- **Allow Transition Time**

Communicating with parents

For infants, toddlers and preschoolers, consider offering A "Look what I did today" sheet every day. Make the use of these forms fun, by copying onto colored paper, adding stickers or your daycare logo.

Let parents know what kind of day their child experienced, if they were happy, fussy, sleepy etc. Monitor the time and amount of food Consumed. Include diaper change times and items needed such as diapers, wipes, extra clothing and formula and/or bottles.

This form also offers a private manner to discuss any concerns or potential problems you may have, without doing so directly in front of the child, other parents or children.

Keep copies of the forms on hand for daily use and complete them throughout the day for accuracy.

Regardless of the age of children you are caring for, keep parents informed. Communicating with parents is an important factor when dealing with them on a day to day basis. Even if you decide not to use this form, communicate with parents on a regular basis.

When presenting parents with a concern or issue, be professional and handle the situation using your best judgment. Encourage parents to discuss their concerns with you as well.

Do not discuss the issues of one family or child with another, this information should be kept confidential.

LOOK WHAT _____DID TODAY

7_____

8_____

9_____

10_____

11_____

12_____

1_____

2_____

3_____

4_____

5_____

I WAS: HAPPY SLEEPY FUSSY
I HAD A: OKAY GREAT TERRIFIC DAY
I ATE: A LOT SOME A LITTLE
I NEED: FORMULA DIAPERS WIPES CLOTHES BOTTLES

DIAPER CHANGES:
8   9   10   11   12   1   2   3   4

COMMENTS: _____

_____

LOOK WHAT _____ DID TODAY

(Circle Those that apply:)

Read/Looked at Books   Blocks   Puzzles   Games   Computer
Arts and Crafts   Outside Play   Dramatic Play   Free Play

COMMENTS: _____

I WAS: HAPPY SLEEPY FUSSY **I HAD A:** OKAY GREAT TERRIFIC DAY **I TOOK A NAP FROM :** _____ TO _____	**I HAD LUNCH AT:** _____ **I HAD SNACKS AT:** _____ AND _____ **I ATE:** A LOT SOME A LITTLE

_____

LOOK WHAT _____ DID TODAY

(Circle Those that apply:)

Read/Looked at Books   Blocks   Puzzles   Games
Computer Activities   Arts and Crafts   Outside Play
Dramatic Play   Free Play _____

I WAS: HAPPY SLEEPY FUSSY **I HAD A:** OKAY GREAT TERRIFIC DAY **I TOOK A NAP FROM :** _____ TO _____	**I HAD LUNCH AT:** _____ **I HAD SNACKS AT:** _____ AND _____ **I ATE:** A LOT SOME A LITTLE

COMMENTS: _____

_____

~Notes~

To get all the forms in this book in an editable form so you can customize them to your daycare visit:

www.DaycareHotline.com/Forms

Copyright 2008-2013 Daycare Systems LLC

Schedules and Activities

Copyright 2008-2013 Daycare Systems LLC

Establishing a Schedule

By establishing a daily routine or schedule, daycare days will be more productive and less chaotic.

The parents you provide care for, will follow a daily schedule, and should be arriving at your home at the same time each morning and evening. Use these times to assist you in planning your routine.

During the course of the day you will have many hours to fill. By having a daily routine, those hours will come to an end, having accomplished the activities you have planned.

Several sample schedules are on the following page. Use them as a guide, to create your own daily schedule.

Following a regular schedule will offer stability to the children and once established, the children will often "watch" the clock more closely than you, ready to start their art project, have a snack, take a nap or play outside.

Think like a parent, when creating your schedule. What activities would you like your children to complete during the day?

When planning your day, consider what activities can be completed during the time allotted? What preparation if any is needed?

Don't get discouraged if you get off schedule…..you can always pick up where you left off the following day.

Once you have completed your Daily Schedule, post it in a visible location. Follow it and make the necessary revisions, until you have created a schedule you can repeat on a regular basis.

Copyright 2008-2013 Daycare Systems LLC

Sample Daycare Schedules

Scheduled Meals, Naps and Activities

7-9   Arrival Time and Free Play
9:00   Scheduled Activity
9:30   Snack
10:00   Free Play
10:30   Scheduled Activity
11.30   Story Time
12:00   Lunch
1:00   Nap or Quiet Time
3:00   Free Play
3:30   Snack
4:00   Scheduled Activity
5:00   The Big Clean Up-Get Ready to Go Home

Scheduled Meals and Naps with the Rest of the Day FREE PLAY

9:30   Snack
Noon   Lunch
1:00   Naps and/or Quiet Time
3:30   Snack
5.00   Big Clean Up-Get ready to go Home

Learning Environment Daycare Setting

8:15   Morning "snack"
9:00   Circle Time / Learning Boards
9:45   Movement Activity
10:15   Free Play
11.00   Art Project or Coloring or Cooking
11:45   Lunch
12:30   Story Time
1:00   Nap or Quiet Time
3:00   Free Play
3:30   Snack
4:00   Free Play and/or Outdoor Activities/Coloring
5:00   The Big Clean Up and Get ready to go home

Copyright 2008-2013 Daycare Systems LLC

What type of Schedule will you choose for your Daycare?

Daycare Schedule	
7:00	
8:00	
9:00	
10:00	
11:00	
12:00	
1:00	
2:00	
3:00	
4:00	
5:00	

Copyright 2008-2013 Daycare Systems LLC

Daycare Schedule

7:00	
8:00	
9:00	
10:00	
11:00	
12:00	
1:00	
2:00	
3:00	
4:00	
5:00	

Activities

As mentioned earlier, the activities you choose, should be age appropriate, encourage movement, creativity, as well as social, gross and fine motor skills.

Gross motor skills are developed through large muscle movement such as walking, dancing, running, jumping, crawling, throwing and kicking.

Fine motor skills are developed through the use of the hands by cutting, pasting, play dough, coloring, blocks, Manipulatives and other hand and eye coordination activities.

Keep the activities and art projects simple, so you can enjoy providing them and the children can easily complete them.

Your participation in the activities, such as story time, circle time and other activities, will encourage the children to interact as a group. This also allows you to become a model for learning.

Encourage the children to share, take turns, and treat the daycare toys, equipment, art supplies and each other with respect.

Before switching from one activity to the next, ask the children to put away the activity they have just finished. This will provide more room for the children to play and reduce trips and falls.

Every night before sending the children home, have them assist you in picking up any toys or activities not in their place.

One way to encourage participation, is to assign a bucket or basket for each child. (A small plastic pail, with their name printed on the side will do). Start singing the clean up song, as they fill their clean up buckets.

Offer stickers as a reward for participation, and the Good Job Jar to promote group participation. Instructions are on **page 106.**

A list of age appropriate activities is located on **page 42.**

Copyright 2008-2013 Daycare Systems LLC

When choosing activities, consider basing them on a Monthly Theme to simplify shopping and planning.

Examples of Monthly Theme ideas are on the following page.

The stories, art projects and activities you choose, should center around the theme chosen.

Regular visits to the library to check out books, provides a free resource for hours of monthly entertainment for the children and introduces them to reading.

Read interactively with the children by asking questions, What color is this? How many dinosaurs do you see? What will happen next? Which one is big? Which one is small? This will not only encourage them to read, but will make story time more enjoyable.

A monthly trip to the arts and crafts store and/or learning store will not only offer you the opportunity to purchase items needed for projects, but will also provide endless ideas for new ones.

Play dough and color books can provide endless hours of creativity and entertainment for the children, and should be offered on a daily basis.

You can make the activities and art projects, as simples or as elaborate as you like, most of all, keep it fun for the kids.

Activity Tips:

- Purchase only washable markers and paint
- Sponges are a great tool for younger children and can be purchased precut in various sizes, shapes, numbers and letters
- For really messy projects have the children wear paint smocks or an old shirt
- If needed, line the table with a vinyl tablecloth or newspaper
- Keep art supplies unavailable to children unless supervised

Monthly Themes

Dinosaurs
- What do dinosaurs eat?
- Do they still exist?
- What colors are they?
- Do they lay eggs?
- What sounds do they make?
- Do they swim? Fly?

Zoo Animals
- What animals live in a zoo?
- What color are they?
- What sounds do they make?
- What do they eat?
- Which ones lay eggs?
- Which ones fly, swim?

Farm Animals
- What animals live on a farm?
- What color are they?
- What sounds do they make?
- What do they eat?
- Which ones fly, swim?
- Where does milk come from?
- Where do eggs come from?

Creatures of the Sea
- What creatures live in the sea?
- Do they lay eggs?
- How big are they?
- What do they eat?

Seasons
- Winter, Summer, Fall, and Spring
- Appropriate Clothing?
- What is the difference between the seasons?

Family
- Who are the members of your family?
- How many brothers do you have?
- How many sisters you have?
- What are their names?
- What color are their eyes and hair?
- Are they tall or short?

Me
- What is your name?
- How old are you?
- What color are your eyes? Hair?
- What is your favorite food? animal?
- Color? Number?
- Body Parts– Head, shoulders, knees, toes, eyes, ears, mouth, nose
- Feelings-What makes you happy, sad, mad?
- Caring and Sharing

People at Work
- What do you want to be when you grow up?
- What are your parent's jobs?
- What tools or equipment would you use for that job?
- When do people work?
- What do they do when they work?
- What kinds of clothes do they where to work-uniforms?

Holidays
Opposites
Alphabet
Numbers
Color
Shapes

Copyright 2008-2013 Daycare Systems LLC

Weekly Activities

Have a special activity planned, at least once per week

Baking Day
- Have the kids gather around the mixing bowl and take turns adding the ingredients
- Mix and bake cookies, bread or?
- Roll out cookies can be cut and baked ahead of time for frosting and decorating
- Bread dough can be divided up for each child and rolled into a variety of shapes and baked

Watch a Video
Limit TV Viewing to 30-60 minutes per day, or not at all.
Choose one day a week as Movie day and take a vote as to what is viewed.

Walk Chalk
Only offer this if you have a safe place to allow the children to draw freely. Don't get it wet and remember it is messy!!

Go for a walk
Walk around the neighborhood or around the block. Have a scavenger hunt in your back yard, look for leaves, talk about the weather, animals, plants.

Plan a Field Trip to the:
Police Station, Fire Station, Post Office, Museum, Park, Zoo, Bank Nursing Home, Children's Hospital, Library, Farm, Pumpkin Patch, Petting Zoo, Bakery or Grocery Store.

Bring the Field Trip to you:
Contact any of the above and ask them to visit your home daycare to offer information regarding their jobs, fire safety, personal safety, etc.

Copyright 2008-2013 Daycare Systems LLC

Everyday Activities

Movement Activities

Inside
- Exercise along with a video or to music
- Sing a Long videos can be a great aid to encourage the kids to sing, dance and move around
- Play musical chairs
- Turn on the stereo and give each of the kids a wooden spoon to use as a microphone and let them perform
- Play dress up
- Have a puppet show

Outside
- Go for a walk
- Set up a scavenger or egg hunt in your back yard
- Free Play
- Play a game, i.e. hide and seek, Simon says, Red Light Green Light, Duck Duck Goose Goose, etc.
- Play soccer, t-ball or basketball
- Blow bubbles

Quiet Activities
- Teach the kids how to play a card or board game
- Build a fort under the kitchen table
- Make cookies or bread dough creations
- If a holiday is coming up, let them help you decorate your home
- Plant flower or vegetable seeds. Measure growth by marking a craft stick or straw
- Read stories or make up stories
- Color
- Finger paint or sponge paint
- Play dough
- Cut and Paste

Copyright 2008-2013 Daycare Systems LLC

Imagination Activities

Post Office

1 medium size cardboard box (large enough to insert and hold envelopes)
scissors
construction paper
envelopes
paper
stickers or blank sticker sheets
Cut a whole in the top of the box for a mail slot. Cover the box with construction paper and label POST OFFICE.
Have the children draw or write letters to each other, address the envelopes and apply stickers in place of stamps.
Appoint one child as the Postman and deliver the mail to the children.

Library

Ask the children to gather into a circle or the reading area. Provide an assortment of books and allow each child to choose a one. Read each child's book out loud. Ask questions while reading, "what do you think will happen next?", "What color is her shirt?" Appoint one child as the Librarian and have the children pretend checking out books and reading them quietly. For older children, encourage them to read out loud.

Music Band

paper plates
dry beans
stapler
if available, paper streamers
crayons or markers
Have the children color the back sides of each paper plate. Staple the paper plates together around the edges, with the top sides facing each   other.   Leave an opening at the top to add the beans. If using streamers, insert in between plates prior to stapling. Staple the top and outer edges to prevent beans from falling out. Allow the children to make up songs and play their tambourines.

Holidays

Halloween Party

Encourage the kids to dress up or bring their costumes. If you prefer the children leave costumes at home, paint their faces or make masks from construction paper. Gather in a circle and tell or read Halloween stories.

Thanksgiving Party

Make Pilgrim and Indian Head Pieces/Hats out of Construction Paper and help the children act out the First Thanksgiving.

Ask the kids how you bake a turkey, write down their response and share with parents. Assemble a Thanksgiving meal for a needy family by having each child bring an item from home.

Christmas Party

Prepare your favorite sugar cookie recipe. Roll and cut out the largest Christmas tree you can find, bake and cool. Provide frosting, sprinkles and baked cookies for each child. Allow them to decorate.

Serve milk with their decorated cookies for snack and allow them to take their creations home.

Valentine Party

Encourage the children to wear red. Serve "heart shaped" sandwiches (cut with a cookie cutter), red juice or punch. Exchange valentines, which can be made earlier in the week.

Easter Egg Hunt

Hold an Easter egg hunt with plastic eggs, filled with age appropriate candy, gum, toys, stickers etc. Allow the children to take home their prizes.

Birthdays

Make each child's day special. Make a paper crown with the child's name and age. Bake cupcakes or a pan cookie and frost, to serve at snack time.

Copyright 2008-2013 Daycare Systems LLC

Craft Recipes

Home-made Play dough

2 Cups Water   2T Oil   4 tsp. Cream of Tartar
1 Cup Salt   2 Cups Flour

Mix all ingredients EXCEPT FLOUR, together in a large heavy saucepan. Stir continuously for approximately 5 minutes over low-med. heat. Add whatever color of food coloring you'd like the dough to be. Gradually stir in the flour. Mixing constantly until dough forms a ball.
Remove from heat and allow to cool. Makes about 4 cups and keeps about 4 weeks in an air tight container.

No Mess Finger Paints

1 ziplock sandwich bag per child (only use extremely durable bags!!)
1 can of shaving cream   food coloring   super glue

Squirt one tennis ball size of shaving cream in each bag. Add a few drops of food coloring. Squeeze out the air out of the bag.   Seal and Super glue. Once the glue has dried give to each child. Show them how to run their fingers around the bag and make swirls and different colors.

Bread Dough Creations

1 loaf thawed bread dough

Cut bread dough into 16 pieces.
Allow the children to form shapes, letters, numbers, snakes, etc. from thawed dough.
When the creations are complete, brush lightly with water and sprinkle with kosher salt, cinnamon and sugar, or grated parmesan cheese.
Bake according to directions on package. Eat when cool!

The Good Job Jar

To encourage good behavior and emphasis on the positive,
establish a good job jar.

Any clear jar with a lid will do. Each day that a child in your care
has a good day, following rules, sharing, good manners, etc., place
a coin, sticker or poker chip, in the jar. (one for each child)

Set a monthly goal for the number of tokens earned. Celebrate their
good behavior, by doing or buying something special, if your goal is met.

Monthly Calendar Instructions

Use one large piece of Poster board.
Use a yard stick to draw the calendar lines.
You will need 7 squares across and 5 squares down.
Leave enough room at the top of the poster board to add the name
of the month. Write the name of the month across the top.
Number and write out the days of the week.

Add birthdays, holidays, field trips, special activity days, or planned
projects. Dates for fire drills and disaster evacuation drills should also
be noted.

Allow the children to decorate the calendar to match your monthly focus,
theme, seasons and/or Holidays.

Use the calendar during circle time to discuss the months, seasons,
yesterday, today and tomorrow, etc.

Paint Smocks

One Large Hand Towel or One Small Bath Towel

Fold Towel in half and cut 1/2 of one circle on fold line. Cut a 4-6 inch slit
from the fold on the back side, just long enough to slip over a child's
head easily. Either machine or hand stitch the circle and slit.

Copyright 2008-2013 Daycare Systems LLC

Learning games

Circle Time is a great way to start off the day. The kids are usually full of energy and ready to start an activity.

Have everyone gather into a circle. Start off with a game of "If you're Happy and You Know It ", "Simon Says" or similar movement games to burn off excess energy.

Remaining in a circle, have the children sit on the floor, criss cross applesauce and play the following games:

Color Game:
Point to each color on the Color Learning Board and ask each child to name the colors. Ask each child what color they are wearing.

Shape Game:
Point to the different shapes on the Shapes Learning Board and ask each child to name the shapes. Search for and point out objects in your home that are of different shapes-i.e. squares-windows, circles-an orange, rectangle-doors etc

Number Game:
Point to the numbers on the Numbers Learning Board and ask each child to state the names of the numbers. Ask each child how old they are and point to the appropriate numbers on the board. Count how many children are in the circle.

Alphabet Game
Sing the Alphabet Song. Then point to each child and say their name and the letter of the alphabet their name starts with. Point these letters out on the Alphabet Learning Board.

Sing other nursery rhymes.

For the last half of Circle Time give each child one of the Learning Boards and Matching Flash cards. Assist them in matching the colors, numbers , shapes and letters. Instructions for all 4 Learning Boards are on the following pages.

These boards can also be used as a game. Gather the children into a circle. Use one of the boards and have them take turns guessing the appropriate matching color, number, letter or shape.

Learning Board Instructions

Materials
Poster Board 4 pieces for smaller boards/8 pieces for large
Colored Construction Paper
Scissors
Glue
Felt Tip Markers

For smaller boards, cut 1 piece of Poster Board in half, making one slightly larger to leave room for the heading. (i.e. Colors, Shapes, etc.) The object is to use one board, as the base and the others for flash cards. Examples and instructions are on the following pages.

Tips
Have the boards laminated, prior to cutting. You could also make a board for each child and allow them to decorate them, before laminating.

Use a large colored felt pen for writing.

Copyright 2008-2013 Daycare Systems LLC

ALPHABET

A	B	C	D	E
F	G	H	I	J
K	L	M	N	O
P	Q	R	S	T
U	V	W	X	Y
		Z		

ALPHABET BOARD

1) Label 1 of the Boards ALPHABET
2) Write out all the letters of the alphabet on this board, it will be used as the base.
3) Write out all the letters of the alphabet on the other board, and cut out each of the letters to create the flash cards.

NUMBERS

1	2	3	4	5
6	7	8	9	10
11	12	13	14	15
16	17	18	19	20

NUMBERS BOARD

1) Label 1 of the Boards NUMBERS
2) Write out the NUMBERS 1-20 on this board, it will be used as the base.
3) Write out the NUMBERS 1-20 on the other board, and cut out each of the letters to create the flash cards.

Copyright 2008-2013 Daycare Systems LLC

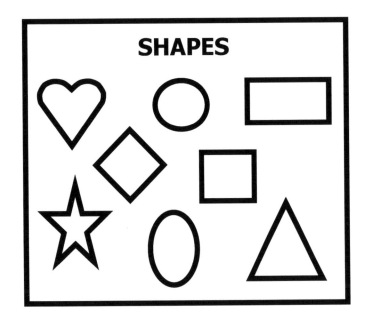

SHAPES BOARD
1) Label 1 of the boards SHAPES
2) Cut out all the shapes from construction paper and glue them on each board or Hand draw them with a markers.
3) Cut the shapes from one board for flash cards and keep the other in tact for the base.

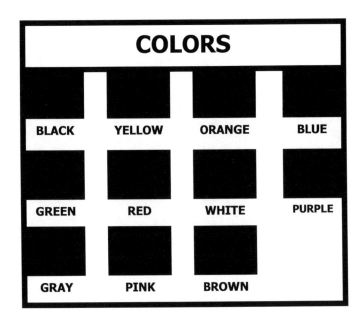

COLOR BOARD
1) Label 1 of the boards COLORS
2) Cut out colored construction paper squares of each color and glue them on both boards
3) Below each color square write out the name of each color
4) Cut the colors from the other board to create the flash cards

Copyright 2008-2013 Daycare Systems LLC

Chapter

10

Daycare Forms

The following forms can be found throughout this book, only those highlighted below are included in this section:

- **Calendar (page 116, 117)**
- **Attendance Record Sheet (page 118)**
- Family Childcare Contract w/3 payment options (page 58-60)
- Childcare Enrollment Information and Authorization Form (56,57)
- Permission to Apply Sunscreen (page 61)
- Permission to Administer Medication (page 66)
- Permission to Transport (page 28)
- Field Trip Permission Slip (page 27)
- Educational Program Permission Slip (page 29)
- Extra Activities Permission Slip (page 29)
- Pre-care Visit Authorization (page 61)
- Accident Report (page 69)
- Interview Checklist (page 54)
- Weekly Meal Planner (page 79-81)
- Grocery List (page 82)
- Look What I did today Sheet (page 90,91)
- Direct Expense Ledger (page 131)
- Indirect Expense Ledger (page 130)
- Grocery Expense Ledger (page 133,134)
- Monthly Income Ledger (page 129)
- General Ledger (page 128)
- Mileage Log (page 127)
- Year End Statement (page 132)
- **Late Notice (page 120)**
- **Payment Increase Notice (page 120)**
- **Termination Notice (page 120)**
- Sample Schedule (page 95)
- Sample Flyer (page 48)
- Sample Announcement Letter (page 49)
- **Photograph Authorization (page 119)**
- **Permission to participate in Water Related Activities (page 119)**
- **I was a Super Star Today (page 121)**

Copyright 2008-2013 Daycare Systems LLC

Daycare Forms

The forms you choose to use in your daycare home, will outline
your rules and regulations, payment policies and authorizations.

The state in which you are licensed, may have specific guidelines
as to the content of your forms, and the length of time in which you
keep completed forms. If your state does not have such a guideline
keep copies of the forms for a minimum of three years, even for those
children you are no longer caring for.

At the end of each year, and/or when you are notified of a change in
address or employment by a daycare family, have a new enrollment
authorization form completed and signed.

In order for the forms to protect you as a provider, you must
enforce all the rules and regulations and/or follow any authorizations
signed by the parents. The signed forms will be the written agreements
between you and your daycare families. Provide copies of the signed
forms to the parents and maintain the originals for your files. Your
licensing agency may request copies, be sure you are in compliance.

Review all the forms carefully and make any additions and or
changes, you feel necessary for you business.

If using the forms as provided confirm they contain all the information
required by your state licensing agency. Complete the appropriate
information on each form, prior to copying. Instructions are located
on the following pages.

There are no graphics on any of the forms in this book, so they
can be customized for your daycare. Copy on colored paper, letterhead,
add stickers, or copy and paste graphics to fit your needs.

Copyright 2008-2013 Daycare Systems LLC

Forms Instructions

MAKE COPIES OF ALL FORMS, PRIOR TO EDITING OR COMPLETING

Calendar
Complete month and dates accordingly. Track absences, field trips, activities, emergency plan practices i.e. fire drills, disaster drills.

Attendance Records
Heading:
Complete name of month and year, child's First and Last Name.
Date, Time and Signature:
Require parents to sign in and out each day.
Hours:
Whether you charge by the hour, week or day, keep track of the number of hours that children are in your care. This can assist you in determining business use of your home and assessing late fees.
Total √ Paid and Total Due for the Week:
Use this column to total each day's earnings. Once payment is received place a check beside the total due, to confirm payment was received.
Additional Charges:
Fill in late fees, NSF charges, overtime, etc.
Balance Carried over from previous month and to following month:
Use these columns only when a week is carried over into the following month. Never continue providing care for someone who does not pay on   time!
Total Paid for Month:
At the end of the month record the totals on the Monthly Income Ledger.
Family Childcare Contract
Complete blanks accordingly, filling in your name, fees, closure dates and rules. Sign where indicated.
Provide a copy to the parents once signed.
Enrollment and Authorization Form
Complete your name (provider) on the first line and date of entry.
Have one form completed per child.

Copyright 2008-2013 Daycare Systems LLC

Payment Increase, Late Notice and Termination
Use accordingly

Authorization Forms
Complete your name (provider), dates and other information according to form. A new authorization form should be completed each time a service is provided i.e., transportation, field trips, medication, photography, water activities. Authorizations for Sunscreen and Enrollment should be renewed each year.

Weekly and Monthly Meal Planners
Complete each week or month and post in a visible location, for easy reference.

Ledgers
Instructions and Bookkeeping Forms are found on **pages 126-135.**

Once the forms have been completed with your names, fees, closure dates, etc., create enrollment packets to have available for Interviews.

Enrollment Packets should include:
- Family Childcare Contract
- Enrollment and Authorization Form (one for each child)
- Sunscreen Permission Slip
- Food Program Documents (if any)
- Permission to Transport, (if providing this service)
- Permission to participate in "Learning Program" (if providing)
- Any other authorizations or forms that apply
- Rules (if on a separate form)

Prior to providing care, make sure that all the forms are completed, signed, and dated. A separate enrollment and authorization form should be completed for each child. Keep the originals and provide copies for the parents.

Create a file for each family, so you can refer to any of the forms at a later date.

Copyright 2008-2013 Daycare Systems LLC

Monday	Tuesday	Wednesday	Thursday	Friday

Copyright 2008-2013 Daycare Systems LLC

					Sunday
					Monday
					Tuesday
					Wednesday
					Thursday
					Friday
					Saturday

Copyright 2008-2013 Daycare Systems LLC

DAYCARE ATTENDANCE RECORD

Month of _____ For _____

Date	Time	Signature	Time	Signature	Hours	Total √ Paid
BALANCE CARRIED OVER FROM PREVIOUS MONTH						$

ADDITIONAL CHARGES				TOTAL DUE FOR WEEK		

ADDITIONAL CHARGES				TOTAL DUE FOR WEEK		

ADDITIONAL CHARGES				TOTAL DUE FOR WEEK		

ADDITIONAL CHARGES				TOTAL DUE FOR WEEK		

ADDITIONAL CHARGES				TOTAL DUE FOR WEEK		
				TOTAL PAID FOR MONTH		
				TOTAL CARRIED OVER TO FOLLOWING MONTH		

Copyright 2008-2013 Daycare Systems LLC

PHOTOGRAPHY AUTHORIZATION

My child _____ may be photographed on

_____ (datc) by _____ (provider)

for _____.

_____
Parent Signature   Date

PERMISSION TO PARTICIPATE IN WATER RELATED ACTIVITIES

My child _____ may participate in water related
activities on _____(date).

_____
Parent Signature   Date

LATE NOTICE

This notice is to inform you, that your payment for Childcare is past due.

As stated in your contract, you will be assessed charges of $ _____ per day until paid in full.

Childcare will not be available again until payment is received.

_____
Provider Signature   Date

RATE INCREASE NOTICE

This notice is to inform you that effective _____ (date) your childcare rate will be increased by $_____ per day/week/hour.

Thank you for your cooperation.

_____
Provider Signature   Date

TERMINATION NOTICE

This notice is to inform you that as of _____ (date) Childcare will no longer be available for _____ (child's name)

_____
Provider Signature   Date

Copyright 2008-2013 Daycare Systems LLC

_____

was a Super Star Today

because _____

_____

_____

was a Super Star Today

because _____

_____

Copyright 2008-2013 Daycare Systems LLC

~NOTES~

To get all the forms in this book in an editable form so you can customize them to your daycare visit:
www.DaycareHotline.com/Forms

Copyright 2008-2013 Daycare Systems LLC

Bookkeeping and Receipts

Copyright 2008-2013 Daycare Systems LLC

Bookkeeping

Refer to Chapter 1, **page 13** for bookkeeping and tax questions, to ask your licensed tax professional.

The following is an example of the items you **may** be able to deduct as business expenses, some of which can be found on the Indirect and Direct Expense Ledgers found in this section:

Direct Expenses
- Educational Supplies
- Business Mileage
- Daycare Groceries
- Books and Toys
- Advertising
- Bank Charges
- Training and Licensing Fees
- Liability Insurance

Indirect Expenses
- Homeowners Insurance
- Property Taxes
- Utility Bills
- Mortgage Interest
- Tax Preparation Fees
- Household Supplies
- Home Improvements

The ledgers contained in this book will keep your income and expenses readily available for calculating quarterly and year end taxable income. Theses ledgers and mileage log should be provided to your Tax Professional at the end of the year, in addition to any other documents they request.

A licensed professional can assist you in calculating additional deductions, including but not limited to: the deductible percentage of indirect expenses; depreciation on your home and equipment; large purchases used for your home and business; quarterly taxes; etc.

For an additional tax advantage, consider opening a self contributing retirement account. Not only will this reduce the amount of taxes you pay, it will be a contribution to your future.

The information in this section is not a substitute for professional Tax or Bookkeeping advice, nor is it an interpretation of any of tax laws. It is highly recommended that you seek the advice of a licensed professional regarding this subject matter, before and for the duration of operating your business.

Copyright 2008-2013 Daycare Systems LLC

Receipts

To adequately maintain your receipts and records, you will need to:

1) Open a separate checking account for business use only

2) Contact a bookkeeper or tax consultant

3) Purchase a 12 pocket month to month receipt folder

As you make purchases, record them in your check book register and on the General ledger found on **page 128.**

Keep receipts for every item purchased or bill paid. Prior to filing receipts, make sure they are itemized. If they do not list the items you purchased or the vendors name and date. Write this information on the receipt yourself.

At the end of the month, transfer the monthly totals from the General Ledger on to the Direct Expense Ledger provided on **page 131.** As you pay utility bills, taxes and other Indirect Expense items, record them on the Indirect Expense Ledger.

A month to month 12 pocket receipt folder is the most efficient way to organize your receipts. These can be purchased at any office supply store for around $10.00.

File all utility bills, grocery receipts, monthly attendance sheets, monthly ledger sheets, bank statements and any other receipts in the receipt folder pocket for the appropriate month.

Keep a mileage log in your vehicle at all times. Use it regularly to track mileage to the grocery store, art/crafts store, field trips, toy store, school pickups and any other use of your vehicle for your business.

At the end of the year, keep tax records, mileage logs and receipts filed together.

Ledger Instructions

General Ledger
A general ledger should be used monthly to track individual expenses, the date those items were purchased and the check number. At the end of each month, record the monthly totals from the general ledger onto the Direct Expense Ledger.

Direct Expense Ledger
Direct Expenses are those expenses related only to your business. Complete this ledger at the end of each month.

Indirect Expense Ledger
Indirect Expenses are those expenses shared by your family and your business. Utility Bills are one such example. Complete the total amount of all items paid, then calculate the percentage you can deduct. To estimate the percentage of business use for your home, see the following calculation worksheet.

Number of hours in a year (365 days x 24 hours in a day)	8760

Number of hours home is available for daycare
(220 days x 10 hours per day*)   2200
*This is the number of hours you are open each day and should include preparation time.

Divide 2200 by 8760
Yearly percentage of time home is available for daycare   25%
(This is the amount of monthly utility bill you can write off)

The above is an example based on using your entire home for your Daycare. Ask your Tax professional for a business use of home worksheet, or provide them with the hours of operation and square footage of your home, and allow them to calculate these figures for you.

Monthly Income Ledger
Record the totals paid by each family each month. This information is located on the Attendance Sheet.

Year End Statement
At the end of every year, provide each family with a Year End Statement, showing how much they paid for the year, your name address, phone number and social security number. The year end totals paid by each family, can be found on your Income Ledger.

Note: Phone expenses do not include costs for your home phone line. This line is for calculating call waiting, voice messaging and other services.

Copyright 2008-2013 Daycare Systems LLC

Mileage Log

Month _____ Year _____

Date	Reason for Trip	Beginning Mileage	Ending Mileage	Total Miles
Total				

Copyright 2008-2013 Daycare Systems LLC

General Ledger

Name: _____

Month: _____ **Year:** _____

Date/ Check #	Advertising	Miscellaneous	Toys	Licenses Dues, Subscriptions	Provider Education Costs	Books Education Supplies	Liability Insurance	Equipment Furniture	Daycare Repairs	Total

www.DaycareHotline.com   Copyright 2008-2013 Daycare Systems LLC

Income Ledger
Year: _____

FAMILY/MONTH	FAMILY	FAMILY	FAMILY	FAMILY	FAMILY	FAMILY	MONTHLY TOTALS
JANUARY							
FEBRUARY							
MARCH							
APRIL							
MAY							
JUNE							
JULY							
AUGUST							
SEPTEMBER							
OCTOBER							
NOVEMBER							
DECEMBER							
YEARLY TOTALS							

Copyright 2008-2013 Daycare Systems LLC

Indirect Expense Ledger
Year: ____

MONTH/ EXPENSE	JAN	FEB	MAR	APRIL	MAY	JUNE	JULY	AUG	SEPT	OCT	NOV	DEC	TOTALS
Phone*													
Power													
Water													
Sewer													
Garbage													
Cable													
Gas													
Rent													
Homeowner Ins.													
Household Repairs													
Household Supplies													
Property Tax													
Totals													
X % Deductible													
TOTALS													

* Phone Expense is for recording call waiting, caller id, voice messaging and other services. Your direct home phone line is not an allowable expense

Copyright 2008-2013 Daycare Systems LLC

Direct Expense Ledger
Year: _____

MONTH/EXPENSE	JAN	FEB	MAR	APRIL	MAY	JUNE	JULY	AUG	SEPT	OCT	NOV	DEC	TOTAL
Advertising													
Supplies													
Toys													
Licensing Fees													
Subscriptions													
Classes/Education													
Books/Educational Supplies													
Liability Insurance													
Equipment/Furniture													
Daycare Repairs													
Bank Charges													
TOTALS													

Copyright 2008-2013 Daycare Systems LLC

Year End Statement

Care provided for:

Parents: _____

Children: _____

Care provided from _____ **to** _____ , _____
(Dates)

Amount Paid: _____
(Total for year)

Providers Name: _____

Providers Social Security Number: _____

Providers Address: _____

_____

Phone Number: _____

Copyright 2008-2013 Daycare Systems LLC

Grocery Expense List Instructions

Column A
Enter Total Number of Meals Served Your Family
3 meals per day x 4 family members = 12 x 30 days
in a month   360

Column B
Enter Total Number of Meals Served Daycare
2 snacks + 1 meal = 2 meals per day per child
2 meals x 4 children = 8 meals per day x 20 days
in a month   160

Column C
Total Meals served in the Month   520

Column D
Divide Number in Column B by Amount in Column C   30.8%

Column E
Total Grocery Expense for the Month $700

Column E
Multiply Column E by Column D $700 x 30.8%

Column F
Total Daycare % of Grocery Expense $215.60

Enter this amount on Direct Expense Ledger

Note If you participate in a Food Program, check their requirements to see if you have to keep your daycare food separate from that of your family's. If you have to keep the food separate, DO NOT USE this form. Consult a licensed tax professional for advice on keeping track of and calculating your grocery expenses for your daycare.

Copyright 2008-2013 Daycare Systems LLC

Grocery Expense Ledger
Year: _____

INSTRUCTIONS /MONTH	JAN	FEB	MARCH	APRIL	MAY	JUNE	JULY	AUG	SEPT	OCT	NOV	DEC	TOTAL
(A) TOTAL # OF MEALS SERVED TO FAMILY													
(B) TOTAL # OF MEALS SERVED TO DAYCARE													
(C) ADD (A) AND (B) TOTAL MEALS SERVED													
(D) DIVIDE (B) MEALS SERVED TO DAYCARE BY (C) TOTAL MEALS SERVED TO DAYCARE AND FAMILY = %													
(E) TOTAL MONTHLY GROCERY BILL													
MULTIPLY (E) TOTAL GROCERY BILL BY (D) %													
THIS % = THE DEDUCTIBLE AMOUNT OF DAYCARE GROCERY EXPENSE													

www.DaycareHotline.com   Copyright 2008-2013 Daycare Systems LLC

Miscellaneous

Any items previously owned and now used exclusively for Daycare purposes

Item   **Present Value**

_____

_____

_____

_____

_____

_____

_____

_____

Any items purchased for use by both your Daycare Business and Family

Date   **Item**   **Cost**

_____

_____

_____

_____

_____

_____

_____

_____

Before making any large purchases, check with your licensed Tax Professional to see if it qualifies as a deduction.

~NOTES~

Copyright 2008-2013 Daycare Systems LLC

Chapter

12

Open for Business

Copyright 2008-2013 Daycare Systems LLC

Summary

As you operate your daycare, don't hesitate to make changes in your schedule and activities. Your willingness to be flexible with parent's schedules and the ages of the children you enroll will be a major factor in following those schedules and activities you originally had planned.

Operate your home daycare like a business

- Use forms
- Follow your rules and policies
- Commit only to those services you can provide on a continuous basis
- Stay Organized

This will not only will you earn the respect of your daycare families, your business and personal life operate more smoothly on a daily basis.

Prepare your Home

Have your home ready for Daycare use each and every morning. Keep your house clean and have activities prepared ahead of time. At the end of the day, have the children cleaned up, diapers changed and ready for the parents.

Transition Time

Give yourself and your family time to adjust to your new schedule and to the new personalities you will be inviting into your home.

Allow the daycare children time to adjust to their new environment and your rules. Keep parents informed as to any concerns or questions you may have, especially in the beginning.

Keeping the lines of communication open during the interview and throughout the course of working with parents and their children will help build and maintain healthy relationships.

Follow through

As discussed earlier, follow all the rules you have chosen for your daycare and implement charges when necessary.

Do not allow parents or others, with the exception of licensing agencies, tell you how to operate your business, make changes in your contract, rates or policies.

Copyright 2008-2013 Daycare Systems LLC

This can be a difficult task especially in the beginning, but can make or break the success of your daycare.

Interviewing potential daycare families, offering pre-care visits, enrolling children on a two week trial basis and allowing transition time for new children enrolled in your daycare, should help reduce terminating care at a later date.

Preparing your home and family, establishing policies and procedures, planning and following a daily schedule, providing fun activities and nutritious meals will create a quality daycare environment

Once you have adjusted to your new business schedule, have fun, enjoy your time with your children and your daycare children.

Continue your Education
As your daycare enrollment grows, I encourage you to attend courses on early childhood development, behavior, child abuse and any other courses available through your Resource and Referral, State Licensing Agency or Community College.

Copyright 2008-2013 Daycare Systems LLC

Copyright 2008-2013 Daycare Systems LLC

A

Appendix

Alphabetical Listing of State Licensing Agencies

Copyright 2008-2013 Daycare Systems LLC

ALABAMA

Department of Human Resources
Office of Day Care and Child Development
Family and Children's Services
50 Ripley Street , Montgomery, AL 36130
Phone: (334) 242-1425
Fax: (334) 242-0939

ALASKA

AK Division of Family and Youth Services
P.O. Box 110630, Juneau, AK 99811-0630
Phone: 907-465-3269
Fax: 907-465-3397 or 907-465-3190

ARIZONA

(Caring for more than 5 children):
Department of Health Services
Office of Child Care Licensure
1647 East Morten, Suite 230
Phoenix, AZ 85020
Phone: 602-674-4220
Fax: 602-861-0674

(Caring for 1 - 4 children):
Department of Economic Security
Child Care Administration, Site Code 801A
P.O. Box 6123 , Phoenix, AZ 85005
Phone: (602) 542-4248
Fax: (602) 542-4197

ARKANSAS

Division of Child Care & Early Childhood
Education and Child Care Licensing
P.O. Box 1437, Slot 720
Little Rock, AR 72203-1437
Phone: 501-682-8590
Fax: 501-682-2317

CALIFORNIA

Central Operations Branch
Department of Social Services
Community Care Licensing Division
744 P Street, Mail Stop 19-50
Sacramento, CA 95814
Phone: (916) 324-4031
Fax: (916) 323-8352

COLORADO

Department of Human Services
Division of Child Care Services
1575 Sherman Street, First Floor
Denver, CO 80203-1714
Phone: (303) 866-5958
Fax: (303) 866-4453

CONNECTICUT

Connecticut Department of Public Health
Child Day Care Licensing
410 Capital Avenue, Mail Station 12 DAC
P.O. Box 340308, Hartford, CT 06134-0308
Phone: (860) 509-8045
Fax: (860) 509-7541

DELAWARE

Department of Services for Children Youth
and Families Office of Child Care Licensing
1825 Faulkland Road, Wilmington, DE 19805
Phone: (302) 892-5800
Fax: (302) 633-5112

DISTRICT OF COLUMBIA

Licensing Regulation Administration
Human Services Facility Division
614 H Street, NW, Suite 1003
Washington, DC 20001
Phone: 202-727-7226
Fax: 202-727-7780

Copyright 2008-2013 Daycare Systems LLC

FLORIDA

Department of Children and Families
Family Safety & Preservation
Child Care Services
1317 Winewood Blvd.
Tallahassee, FL 32399-0700
Phone: 850-488-4900
Fax: 850-488-9584

GEORGIA

Department of Human Resources
Office of Regulatory Services
Child Care Licensing Section
2 Peachtree Street, NW
32nd Floor, Room #458
Atlanta, GA 30303-3142
Phone: (404) 657-5562
Fax: (404) 657-8936

HAWAII

Department of Human Services
Benefits, Employment and Support Services
Division
1001 Bishop Street
Pacific Tower, Suite 900
Honolulu, HI 96813
Phone: (808) 586-5770
Fax: (808) 586-5180

IDAHO

Department of Health and Welfare
Bureau of Family and Children's Services
450 West State Street
P.O. Box 83720
Boise, ID 83720-0036
Phone: (208) 334-5691
Fax: (208) 334-6664

ILLINOIS

Department of Children and Family Services
Bureau of Licensure & Certification
406 East Monroe Street - Station 60
Springfield, IL 62701-1498
Phone: (217) 785-2688
Fax: (217) 524-3347

INDIANA

Indiana Family & Social Services
Administration
Division of Family and Children
Bureau of Child Development
Licensing Unit
402 W. Washington Street, Room 386
Indianapolis, IN 46204
Phone: 317-232-4521 or
317-232-1660
Fax: 317-232-4436

IOWA

Department of Human Services
Adult, Children and Family Services
Child Day Care Unit
Hoover State Office Building, 5th Floor
Des Moines, IA 50319
Phone: 515-281-6074
Fax: 515-281-4597

KANSAS

Department of Health and Environment
Child Care Licensing and Registration
109 SW 9th Street
Mills Building, 400-C
Topeka, KS 66612-2218
Phone: (785) 296-1270
Fax: (785) 296-7025

Copyright 2008-2013 Daycare Systems LLC

KENTUCKY

(Caring for 7 or more children)
Cabinet for Health Services Div. of Licensing
C.H.R. Building
275 East Main Street, 4E-A
Frankfort, KY 40621
Phone: 502-564-2800
Fax: 502-564-6546

(Caring for 3-6 children)
No certification needed for up to 3 children
Community Based Services
Division of Child Care
C.H.R. Building, 3EB6
275 East Main Street, Frankfort, KY 40621
Phone: 502-564-2524
Fax: 502-564-9554

LOUISIANA

Department of Social Services
Bureau of Licensing
P.O. Box 3078, Baton Rouge, LA 70821
Phone: (504) 922-0015
Fax: (504) 922-0014

MAINE

Bureau of Child & Family Services
221 State Street, State House, Station 11
Augusta, ME 04333
Phone: 207-287-5060
Fax: 207-287-5031

MARYLAND

Maryland Dept. of Human Resources
Child Care Administration
311 W. Saratoga Street, 1st Floor
Baltimore, MD 21201
Phone: (410) 767-7805
Fax: (410) 333-8699

MASSACHUSETTS

Office of Child Care Services
One Ashburton Place, Room 1105
Boston, MA 02108
Phone: 617-727-8900
Fax: 617-626-2028

MICHIGAN

Department of Consumer & Industry Services
Division of Child Day Care Licensing
7109 W. Saginaw, 2nd Floor
P.O. Box 30650, Lansing, MI 48909-8150
Phone: 517-373-8300
Fax: 517-335-6121

MINNESOTA

(Refers family child care calls to counties)
Department of Human Services
Division of Licensing
444 Lafayette Road
St. Paul, MN 55155-3842
Phone: 612-296-3971
Fax: 612-297-1490

MISSISSIPPI

Department of Health Division of Child Care
P.O. Box 1700, Jackson, MS 39215-1700
Phone: (601) 960-7613
Fax: (601) 354-6131

MISSOURI

Department of Health Bureau of Child Care,
Safety and Licensure
P.O. Box 570 (920 Wildwood)
Jefferson City, MO 65102
Phone: (573) 751-2450
Fax: (573) 526-5345

Copyright 2008-2013 Daycare Systems LLC

MONTANA

Department of Public Health
Quality Assurance Division
Child Care Program
P.O. Box 202951, Helena, MT 59620-2951
Phone: 406-444-2012
Fax: 406-444-1742

NEBRASKA

NE Dept. of Health & Human Services
Child Care
P.O. Box 95044, Lincoln, NE 68509-5044
Phone: 402-471-9431
Fax: 402-471-9455

NEVADA

Department of Human Resources
Division of Child and Family Services
Bureau of Child Care Licensing
3920 E. Idaho Street, Elko, NV 89801
Phone: 702-753-1237
Fax: 702-753-2111

NEW HAMPSHIRE

New Hampshire Department of Health
and Human Services
Office of Program Support
Bureau of Child Care Licensing
6 Hazen Drive, Concord, NH 03301
Phone: 603-271-4624
Fax: 603-271-3745

NEW JERSEY

State of New Jersey Dept. of Human Services
Division of Youth & Family Services,
Bureau of Licensing
PO Box 717 Trenton, NJ 08625-0717
Phone: (609) 292-1018

NEW MEXICO

Child Services Unit / Licensing
PERA Building, Room 111
P.O. Drawer 5160, Santa Fe, NM 87502
Phone: 505-827-4185
Fax: 505-827-7361

NEW YORK

New York State Dept of Family Assistance
Office of Children and Family Services
Bureau of Early Childhood Services
40 N. Pearl Street, 11-B
Albany, NY 12243
Phone: 518-474-9454
Fax: 518-474-9617
**For the 5 boroughs of New York City:
Manhattan, Queens, Brooklyn, Bronx,
and Staten Island**
NY City Dept of Health-Bureau of Day-Care
2 Lafayette Street, 22nd Floor
New York, NY 10007
Phone: 212-676-2444
Fax: 212-676-2424

NORTH CAROLINA

Division of Child Development
Regulatory Services Section
P.O. Box 29553, Raleigh, NC 27626
Phone: (919) 662-4499
Fax: (919) 661-4845
Child Care Resource Center Hotline
(800) CHOOSE-1

NORTH DAKOTA

Human Services Early Childhood Services
600 East Boulevard
State Capitol Bldg, Bismarck, ND 58505
Phone: 701-328-4809
Fax: 701-328-2359

Copyright 2008-2013 Daycare Systems LLC

OHIO

Department of Human Services
Bureau of Workforce Development
Child Day Care Licensing Section
65 East State Street, 2nd Floor
Columbus, OH 43215
Phone: (614) 466-3822
Fax: (614) 728-6803

OKLAHOMA

Oklahoma Department of Human Services
Office of Child Care
4545 N. Lincoln, Suite 100
P.O. Box 25352, Oklahoma City, OK 73105
Phone: (405) 521-3561
Fax: (405) 521-0391

OREGON

Employment Department
Child Care Division
875 Union Street, NE, Salem, OR 97311
Phone: 503-947-1400
Fax: 503-947-1428

PENNSYLVANIA

Pennsylvania Department of Public Welfare
Bureau of Child Day Care Office of Children
Youth & Families, Bertolino Bldg., 4th Floor
P.O. Box 2675, Harrisburg, PA 17105-2675
Phone: (717) 787-8691
Fax: (717) 787-1529

RHODE ISLAND

Department of Children
Youth and Families Day Care Licensing
Building 3, 610 Mount Pleasant Avenue
Providence, RI 02908
Phone: (401) 222-4741

Fax: (401) 457-5331

SOUTH CAROLINA

Department of Social Services
Division of Child Day Care Licensing
P.O. Box 1520
Columbia, SC 29202-1520
Phone: (803) 734-5740
Fax: (803) 734-4322

SOUTH DAKOTA

South Dakota Department of Social Services
Child Care Services
Kneip Building
700 Governors Drive
Pierre, SD 57501-2291
Phone: (605) 773-4766
Fax: (605) 773-6834

TENNESSEE

Tennessee Department of Human Services
Day Care Licensing Unit
Citizens Plaza
400 Deaderick Street
Nashville, TN 37248-9800
Phone: (615) 313-4778
Fax: (615) 532-9956

TEXAS

Department of Protective and
Regulatory Services
Child Care Licensing
P.O. Box 149030
M.C. E-550
Austin, TX 78714
Day Care Hotline:
800-862-5252 or 512-438-3267
Fax: 512-438-3848

Copyright 2008-2013 Daycare Systems LLC

UTAH

Bureau of Licensing
Child Care Unit
P.O. Box 142003
Salt Lake City, UT 84114-2003
Phone: 801-538-9299
Fax: 801-538-9259

VERMONT

Vermont Department of Social and
Rehabilitation Services
Child Care Services Division
Child Care Licensing Unit
103 S. Main Street
Waterbury, VT 05671-2901
Phone: (802) 241-2158
(802) 241-3110
Fax: (802) 241-1220

VIRGINIA

Department of Social Services
Division of Licensing Programs
730 E. Broad Street, 7th Floor
Richmond, VA 23219-1849
Phone: 804-692-1787
Fax: 804-692-2370

WASHINGTON

Washington Department of Social
and Health Services
Office of Child Care Policy
P.O. Box 45700
Olympia, WA 98504-5710
Phone: (360) 902-8038
Fax: (360) 902-7903

WEST VIRGINIA

Department of Health and Human Resources
Day Care Licensing
P.O. Box 2590
Fairmont, WV 26555-2590
Phone: 304-363-3261
Fax: 304-367-2729

WISCONSIN

Division of Children & Family Services
Bureau of Regulation and Licensing
1 West Wilson Street
P.O. Box 8916
Madison, WI 53708-8916
Phone: 608-266-9314
Fax: 608-267-7252

WYOMING

Department of Family Services
Division of Juvenile Services
Hathaway Bldg., Room 323
2300 Capitol Avenue,
Cheyenne, WY 82002-0490
Phone: (307) 777-6285
Fax: (307) 777-3659

**For updated contacted information, visit
the following website:**

http://nrc.uchsc.edu/states.html

Copyright 2008-2013 Daycare Systems LLC

Appendix

Poison Control Centers

Copyright 2008-2013 Daycare Systems LLC

ALABAMA
Alabama Poison Center
(800) 462-0800 (AL only) (205) 345-0600
Regional Poison Control Center
(800) 292-6678 (AL only); (205) 933-4050

ALASKA
(800) 478-3193; (907) 261-3193

ARIZONA
Arizona, except Phoenix
(800) 362-0101 (AZ only); (520) 626-6016
Maricopa County (Phoenix)
(800) 362-0101 (AZ only); (602) 253-3334

ARKANSAS
(800) 376-4766

CALIFORNIA
Fresno/Madera/Central California
(800) 876-4766 (CA only)
Sacramento/Northeast California
(800) 876-4766 (CA only)
San Francisco Bay Area
(800) 876-4766 (CA only)
San Diego County and Imperial County
(800) 876-4766 (CA only)

COLORADO
Rocky Mountain Poison & Drug Center
(800) 332-3073 (CO only/outside metro)
(303) 739-1123 (Denver metro)

CONNECTICUT
Connecticut Poison Control Center
(800) 343-2722 (CT only); (860) 679-3456

DELAWARE
(800) 722-7112; (215) 386-2100

DISTRICT OF COLUMBIA
(202) 625-3333

FLORIDA
Jacksonville/Northern & Eastern Coastal
(800) 282-3171 (FL only); (904) 549-4480
Miami and Surrounding Metro Counties
(800) 282-3171 (FL only); (305) 585-5253
Tampa & Surrounding areas
(800) 282-3171 (FL only); (813) 253-4444

GEORGIA
(800) 282-5846; (404) 616-9000

HAWAII
(808) 941-4411

IDAHO
(800) 860-0620 (ID only)

ILLINOIS
(800) 942-5969 (IL only)

INDIANA
(800) 382-9097 (IN only); (317) 929-2323

IOWA
Iowa Poison Center
(800) 352-2222; (712) 277-2222
Poison Control Center
(800) 272-6477 (IA only)

KANSAS
(800) 332-6633 (KS only); (913) 588-6633

KENTUCKY
(502) 589-8222

LOUISIANA
(800) 256-9822 (LA only

MAINE
(800) 442-6305 (ME only) (207) 871-2950

Copyright 2008-2013 Daycare Systems LLC

MARYLAND
Maryland Poison Center
(800) 492-2414 (MD only); (410) 706-7701
National Capital Poison Center
Washington, DC/surrounding metro
(202) 625-3333

MASSACHUSETTS
(800) 682-9211 (MA only);(617) 232-2120

MICHIGAN
Southeast & Thumb Area
(800) 764-7661 (MI only); (313) 745-5711
Eastern Michigan and Peninsula
(800) 764-7661 (MI only)

MINNESOTA
Minneapolis and Surrounding Counties
(800) POISON1 (MN & SD only)
(612) 347-3141

MISSISSIPPI
(601) 354-7660

MISSOURI
(800) 366-8888; (314) 772-5200
Area Served: Western Missouri
(816) 234-3430

MONTANA
(800) 525-5042 (MT only)

NEBRASKA
(800) 955-9119 (NE & WY only);
(402) 354-5555

NEVADA
Northern Nevada/
(503) 494-8968
Clark & Nye Counties
(800) 446-6179 (NV only)

NEW HAMPSHIRE
(800) 562-8236 (NH only); (603) 650-8000

NEW JERSEY
(800) POISON-1 (NJ only)

NEW MEXICO
(800) 432-6866 (NM only); (505) 272-2222

NEW YORK
Central New York State
(800) 252-5655 (NY only); (315) 476-4766
Finger Lakes Region of New York
(800) 333-0542 (NY only); (716) 275-3232
East Part of New York/NYC-Canada
(800) 336-6997 (NY only); (914) 366-3030
Long Island
(516) 542-2323;(516) 663-2650
(516) 924-8811 (TDD Suffolk)
New York City
(800) 210-3985; (212) 340-4494;
(212) POISONS; (212) VENENOS
Western New York
(800) 888-7655 (NY Western regions only);
(716) 878-7654

NORTH CAROLINA
(800) 848-6946 (NC only); (704) 355-4000

NORTH DAKOTA
(800) 732-2200 (ND, MN, SD only)
(701) 234-5575

OHIO
Central Ohio
(800) 682-7625 (OH only)
(800) 762-0727 (Dayton, OH only)
(614) 228-1323
Southwest Ohio
(800) 872-5111 (OH only); (513) 558-5111
Cleveland & Surrounding Metro
(888) 231-4455 (OH only); (216) 231-4455

Copyright 2008-2013 Daycare Systems LLC

OKLAHOMA
(800) 764-7661 (OK only); (405) 271-5454

OREGON
(800) 452-7165 (OR only); (503) 494-8968

PENNSYLVANIA
Central Pennsylvania
(800) 521 6110; (717) 531-6111
Western Pennsylvania
(412) 681-6669
SE Pennsylvania/Lehigh Valley
(800) 722-7112; (215) 386-2100

PUERTO RICO
(787) 726-5674

RHODE ISLAND
(401) 444-5727

SOUTH CAROLINA
(800) 922-1117 (SC only); (803) 777-1117

SOUTH DAKOTA
(800) POISON1 (MN and SD only)
(612) 347-3141

TENNESSEE
Middle Tennessee
(800) 288-9999 (TN only);
(615) 936-2034 (Greater Nashville)
Western & Eastern Tennessee
(800) 288-9999 (TN only); (901) 528-6048

TEXAS
Central Texas
(800) POISON-1 (TX only); (254) 724-7401
North Texas
Texas Poison Center Network
(800) 764-7661 (TX only)

South Texas
(800) 764-7661 (TX only)
Southeast Texas
(800) 764-7661 (TX only)
Amarillo and Surrounding Area
(800) 764-7661 (TX only)
West Texas
(800) 764-7661 (TX only)

UTAH
(800) 456-7707 (UT only); (801) 581-2151

VERMONT
(877) 658-3456 (toll free); (802) 658-3456

VIRGINIA
Western & Central Virginia
(800) 451-1428 (VA only); (804) 924-5543
Washington, DC & surrounding metro
(202) 625-3333
Eastern and Central Virginia
(800) 552-6337;(804) 828-9123

WASHINGTON
(800) 732-6985 (WA only); (206) 526-2121

WEST VIRGINIA
(800) 642-3625 (WV only)

WISCONSIN
Eastern Wisconsin
(800) 815-8855 (WI only); (414) 266-2222
Western Wisconsin
(800) 815-8855 (WI only); (608) 262-3702

WYOMING
(800) 955-9119 (NE & WY only);
(402) 354-5555

Appendix

Child Abuse Hotlines

Alabama Sheriff's Department	**Kansas** (800) 922-5330	**North Dakota** County Social Services
Alaska (800)478-4444	**Kentucky** (800) 752-6200	**Ohio** District offices of Human Services
Arizona (888) SOS-CHILD/ (888) 767-2445	**Louisiana** Local Child Protective Agency	**Oklahoma** (800) 522-3511
Arkansas (800) 482-5964	**Maine** (800) 452-1999	**Oregon** (800) 854-3508
California State licensing office	**Maryland** (410) 767-7558/(410) 767-651	**Pennsylvania** (800) 932-0313
Colorado Department of Social Services	**Massachusetts** (800) 792-5200	**Rhode Island** (800) 742-4453
Connecticut (800) 842-2288	**Michigan** (800) 942-4357	**South Carolina** Dept. of Social Services
Delaware (800) 292-9582	**Minnesota** (612) 296-3971	**South Dakota** Dept. of Social Services or Local law enforcement
Florida (800) 962-2873	**Mississippi** (800) 222-8000	**Tennessee** County 24-hour "hot line"
Georgia Family and Children's Services	**Missouri** (800) 392-3738	**Texas** (800) 252-5400
Hawaii **Oahu:** (808) 587-5266 **Honolulu:** (808) 622-7111 **Wahiawa:** (808) 959-0669 **Maui:** (808) 242-8418 **Kauai:** (808) 245-3461	**Montana** (800) 332-6100 **Nebraska** (800) 652-1999 **Nevada** (800) 992-5757 **New Hampshire** (800) 894-5533	**Utah** (800) 678-9399 **Vermont** (802) 241-2131 **Virginia** (800) 552-7906 **Washington** (800) 562-5624
Idaho Local Health and Welfare Office	**New Jersey** (800) 792-8610	**West Virginia** (800) 352-6513
Illinois (800) 252-2873	**New Mexico** (800) 432-2075	**Wisconsin** County Social or Human Services or local law agency
Indiana (800) 562-2407	**New York** (800) 342-3720	**Wyoming** Local of Department of Family Services or law enforcement
Iowa (800) 362-2178	**North Carolina** (800) 662-7030	**National Child Abuse Hotline** (800) 422-4453

Copyright 2008-2013 Daycare Systems LLC

Appendix

Associations and other Resources

Copyright 2008-2013 Daycare Systems LLC

Child Care Law Center
973 Market Street, Suite 550
San Francisco, CA 94103
(415) 495-5498
Fax: (415) 495-6734
E-mail: cclc@childcarelaw.com
http://www.childcarelaw.org

National Association of Child Care Resource and Referral Agencies (NACCRRA)
1319 F Street, NW, Suite 810
Washington, DC 20004-1106
(202) 393-5501
Fax: (202) 393-1109
http://www.naccrra.net

ERIC Clearinghouse on Elementary and Early Childhood Education (ERIC/EECE)
University of Illinois, Children's Research
51 Gerty Drive, Champaign, IL 61820-7469
(800) 583-4135 or (217) 333-1386
Fax: (217) 333-3767
http://ericeece.org

International Child Care Business & Technology Association
E-mail: info@iccbta.com
http://www.ICCBTA.com
Plano, TX

National Child Care Information Center
243 Church Street, NW, 2nd Floor
Vienna, VA 22180
(800) 616-2242
Fax: (800) 716-2242
TTY: (800) 516-2242
E-mail: info@nccic.org
http://nccic.org

Association for Early Learning Leaders (formerly NACCP)
8000 Centre Park Drive, Ste. 170
Austin, TX 78754
(800)537 1118
info@earlylearningleaders.org
http://www.naccp.org

National Association for Family Child Care (NAFCC)
1743 W. Alexander Street
Salt Lake City, Utah   84119
Phone: 801-886-2322
Phone: 801-88-NAFCC
Fax: 801-886-2325
Email: nafcc@nafcc.org
http://www.nafcc.org

National Resource Center for Health and Safety in Child Care
University of Colorado Health Sciences
Center at Fitzsimons
National Resource Center for Health and
Safety in Child Care
Campus Mail Stop 6508
Aurora, CO 80044-0508
(800) 598-KIDS
Fax: (303) 315-8660
E-mail: Natl.child.res.ctr.@UCHSC.edu
http://nrc.uchsc.edu

Copyright 2008-2013 Daycare Systems LLC

Resources

Daycare Hotline
A Leading Resource for Daycare Providers
http://www.daycarehotline.com
information@daycarehotline.com
(877) 254-4619

Child Care Center Marketing and Consulting
Grow Your Enrollment in 89 Days or Less...Guaranteed
Kris Murray, President
www.Childcare-Marketing.com
info@childcare-marketing.com
(877) 254-4619

Childcare Insurance Specialist Brokerage
Stephanie Spencer
(800) 273-4510
Morgan and Associates, Inc.
5705 95th Place SW Mukilteo, WA 98275
http://www.morganinsurance.com
info@morganinsurance.com

Tax Specialists—Family Daycare
Sharon Riley
Nelson and Riley, Inc.
Tampa, Florida
http://www.nelsonandriley.biz
(813) 886-9567

Tom Copeland
www.tomcopeland.net
www.tomcopelandblog.com

Index

Since 1997 Daycare Hotline has been dedicated to helping loving people start and manage daycare programs of all sizes—from small home-based programs to large multi-location centers. With a full range of educational and coaching products, there is no other company with the proven knowledge and skills to help you succeed in the daycare business.

Learn what over 2,000 people just like you have already learned. Kris Murray, America's leading expert in child care business, has the knowledge and experience to help ensure your success.

Visit www.DaycareHotline.com to learn more and make sure you start your daycare on the proven path to success.

Visit www.Childcare-Marketing.com to maximize your enrollment and revenue, and take your business to the next level of success.

Copyright 2008-2013 Daycare Systems LLC

Made in the USA
San Bernardino, CA
26 April 2020

69890171R00089